PATHFINDER MODULE

Author · Thurston Hillman
Development Lead · Crystal Frasier
Cover Artist · Craig J Spearing
Interior Artists · Lucas Durham, Sally Gottschalk,
  Kez Laczin, Ian Perks, Andrea Radeck, Lance Red,
  and Anson Tan
Cartographer · Robert Lazzaretti

Creative Director · James Jacobs
Editor-in-Chief · F. Wesley Schneider
Executive Editor · James L. Sutter
Senior Developer · Rob McCreary
Developers · John Compton, Adam Daigle, Mark Moreland,
  and Owen K.C. Stephens
Senior Editors · Judy Bauer and Christopher Carey
Editors · Jason Keeley and Josh Vogt
Lead Designer · Jason Bulmahn
Designers · Logan Bonner, Stephen Radney-MacFarland,
  and Mark Seifter

Managing Art Director · Sarah E. Robinson
Art Director · Sonja Morris
Senior Graphic Designer · Adam Vick
Graphic Designer · Emily Crowell

Publisher · Erik Mona
Paizo CEO · Lisa Stevens
Chief Operations Officer · Jeffrey Alvarez
Director of Sales · Pierce Watters
Sales Associate · Cosmo Eisele
Marketing Director · Jenny Bendel
Vice President of Finance · Christopher Self
Staff Accountant · Ashley Kaprielian
Data Entry Clerk · B. Scott Keim
Chief Technical Officer · Vic Wertz
Software Development Manager · Cort Odekirk
Senior Software Developer · Gary Teter
Project Manager · Jessica Price
Organized Play Coordinator · Tonya Woldridge
Adventure Card Game Designer · Tanis O'Connor

Community Team · Liz Courts and Chris Lambertz
Customer Service Team · Sharaya Copas, Katina Davis,
  Sara Marie Teter, and Diego Valdez
Warehouse Team · Will Chase, Mika Hawkins,
  Heather Payne, Jeff Strand, and Kevin Underwood
Website Team · Christopher Anthony, Lissa Guillet,
  Julie Iaccarino, Erik Keith, and Scott Spalding

On the Cover

A group of angry Mireborn lizardfolk confront Sajan outside of their jungle temple during a raging storm in this dramatic cover art by Craig J Spearing.

Ire of the Storm

Table of Contents

Reference

This book refers to several other Pathfinder Roleplaying Game products using the following abbreviations, though these additional supplements are not required to make use of this book. Readers interested in references to Pathfinder RPG hardcovers can find the complete rules of these books available online for free at **paizo.com/prd**.

Advanced Player's Guide	APG	*Ultimate Magic*	UM
Ultimate Equipment	UE		

paizo

Paizo Inc.
7120 185th Ave NE, Ste 120
Redmond, WA 98052-0577

MODULE

Ire of the Storm

Advancement Track

Ire of the Storm is designed for four characters
and uses the medium XP track.

1   The PCs begin the adventure at 1st level.

2   The PCs should be 2nd level after investigating the
attack at Fort Breakthrough.

3   The PCs should be 3rd level early in their exploration of
the marshlands around Pridon's Hearth.

4   The PCs should be 4th level before entering the Sky
Tempest Temple.

5   The PCs should be 5th level by the time they descend into
the caverns below the Sky Tempest Temple.

6   The PCs should be 6th level at the end of the adventure.

Adventure Summary

In *Ire of the Storm*, the heroes are new arrivals in
the tiny Sargavan colony of Pridon's Hearth, and
are tasked with identifying why the local fort hasn't
reported in. Upon investigating, they discover the militia
slaughtered by unknown parties. The heroes have little
time to respond, though, as Pridon's Hearth needs their
help to prepare for the worsening weather. As the storms
overhead continue to grow, the Mireborn lizardfolk
attack the town and the heroes must set out into the
unexplored surroundings to find the aggressors' lair and
determine their connection to the steadily worsening
tempest. Can they befriend locals, explore lost ruins, and
overcome an Aspis conspiracy, before finally confronting
the Mireborn and their sinister shaman, Daruthek?

Adventure Background

Birthed in the wake of the god Aroden's disappearance, the Eye of Abendego—a massive, endless hurricane that churns along Garund's western coast—destroyed two great nations, but it also gave rise to a number of academics and cults focused on the storm. The Storm Kindlers, devotees of the deity Gozreh, flocked to the Sodden Lands to witness what they thought was the ultimate manifestation of their god's power. These cultists believed that the Eye represented Gozreh's might, will, and intentions, and that those reverent enough could read the future in the weather patterns it produced. The Storm Kindlers established themselves in the storm-wracked land, but their faith could not spare them from the flooding and relentless wind. One by one, the Storm Kindlers who dwelled in the Sodden Lands perished, wiped out by the very natural wonder they gathered to worship.

One sect did manage to escape—ironically, because the Storm Kindlers exiled them as heretics. Led by the ambitious ex-merchant Chitauli, these outcasts believed that they could read the future in the ebb and flow of storms, and that they could seize control of fate by controlling the Eye of Abendego itself. Chitauli's followers developed a number of blasphemous rituals to usurp the natural order that most Gozrens revere. The Storm Kindlers eventually banished the cult, cutting them off from easy access to the Eye, their supposed tool for manipulating destiny. The outcasts journeyed south, passing beyond Sargava and into previously unexplored territories along the Lower Korir River delta.

Far from defeated, Chitauli and his followers saw their new home—far away from their blind and patronizing overseers in the Sodden Lands—as the perfect place to experiment with their beliefs. The exiles constructed a vast edifice of stone dedicated to Gozreh, and they dubbed it the Sky Tempest Temple. Here they resolved to craft their own endless storm from which they could succor the secrets of creation and control fate: the Eye of Gozreh.

Chitauli guided the Storm Kindlers in performing countless rituals, each intended to summon vast storms to the region, but ultimately created little more than tepid rains. These constant failures frustrated the Storm Kindlers; coupled with their isolation from the civilized world and their constant battle against the region's deadly wildlife, many members of the cult began defecting. Desperate to hold together his crumbling power base, Chitauli turned to a vile new master: the evil elemental Lord of Water, Kelizandri. Fueled by the Elemental Planes, the rituals suddenly gained teeth, and the Storm Kindlers began constructing a massive storm engine in a complex below their temple to artificially maintain and enhance their newborn hurricane. But as the Eye of Gozreh began to form, the Storm Kindlers uncovered their leader's horrible truth—Chitauli had rededicated their temple and their very souls to an evil force. The Storm

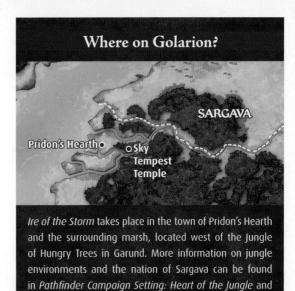

Where on Golarion?

SARGAVA

Pridon's Hearth ○ ○ Sky
Tempest
Temple

Ire of the Storm takes place in the town of Pridon's Hearth and the surrounding marsh, located west of the Jungle of Hungry Trees in Garund. More information on jungle environments and the nation of Sargava can be found in *Pathfinder Campaign Setting: Heart of the Jungle* and *Pathfinder Player Companion: Sargava, the Lost Colony*. Pridon's Hearth is more fully detailed in the gazetteer on page 58.

Kindlers slew their former leader, and without a primary caster to control the ritual, the Eye of Gozreh collapsed, devastating the temple and killing the remaining cultists. Infused with malignant energy, Chitauli's soul survived as a spectre bound to the mechanism he created.

Decades later, the local Mireborn tribe of lizardfolk encountered the ruins. Although they operated primarily north of the delta, the lizardfolk used the ruins as an occasional seasonal encampment. But after decades of being deserted, the trickle of elemental energy within the temple had grown into a magical miasma. Though too mild to affect the adult lizardfolk, it suffused the eggs laid in the temple and led to the birth of a dozen sickly, feather-covered infants, all but one of whom died within weeks. The survivor—Daruthek—eventually manifested strange magical abilities.

A Sargavan prospector named Rema Pridon stumbled across Storm Kindler charts left behind when the cult members purchased supplies in Eleder during their journey south. Pridon set sail after them, convinced that a Gozren cult must be privy to secrets about the region's natural resources. She entrusted the Storm Kindlers' charts to a colleague—who was, unbeknownst to her, a member of the Aspis Consortium—before launching his expedition. Although Pridon soon died, the eventual discovery of her camp sparked renewed interest in the region. The nation of Sargava granted the land to the Narsus family to colonize and manage in Sargava's name. These colonists founded the town of Pridon's Hearth, unaware that the century-old ruins of the Sky Tempest Temple a few dozen miles away still hold the magic to birth an endless hurricane that could wipe out not just their settlement, but the nation of Sargava as well.

CHAPTER 1

The Deluge

After Sargava granted land to his family, the newly titled Count Servius Narsus had no idea that the Aspis Consortium funded much of his original colonization effort, and that the first shipload of arrivals included undercover Aspis agents under the command of Hamsa Gadd. While most settlers were content to stake their claims within or near the safety of Pridon's Hearth's walls, Gadd's orders called for an immediate survey of the surrounding jungle in search of a lost Gozren cult. Only many years later, after the recruiting a Qadiran Storm Kindler named Magdi Kukoyi who was eager to uncover his cult's lost history, did Gadd's explorations pay off: she discovered the temple's ruins deep in the jungle.

Unfortunately for her expedition, after taking a violent thrashing from the neighboring Blackbruise Brood boggards, the Mireborn lizardfolk fell back to their remote camp at the Sky Tempest Temple, only to discover the human infestation. Hamsa Gadd escaped the lizardfolk's wrath and limped back alone to Pridon's Hearth. Unknown to her, Magdi Kukoyi also survived, having parlayed with the tribe's spiritual leader. Swamp-Speaker Daruthek—a lizardfolk oracle conceived inside the temple's walls 20 years earlier, and whose flesh reveals clear signs of planar influence—had studied the temple's inscriptions all his life, but never knew enough about the Storm Kindlers' philosophy to put the pieces together. While he despised Kukoyi's humanity, Daruthek coveted the secrets the man could reveal, and persuaded Chief Shathra to spare him.

The Mireborn soon discovered the new human settlement of Pridon's Hearth, and still smarting from

their territorial dispute with the boggards, resolved to remove the outsiders. The humans' superior numbers, though, made open warfare unattractive. As the lizardfolk debated the matter, Daruthek's interrogations of his prisoner and explorations of the temple's lower level brought him into contact with Chitauli's restless spirit. Where Kukoyi's lessons fell short, Chitauli filled in vital details. Within weeks, Daruthek discovered the details of the ritual once employed by Chitauli's heretic Storm Kindlers, and brought those secrets to his tribe as a means to expel the humans of Pridon's Hearth. Desperate, the Mireborn accepted Daruthek's plan for salvation.

Meanwhile, Hamsa Gadd returned to Pridon's Hearth, omitting her discovery of the Sky Tempest Temple even as she quietly begged her Aspis overseers in Eleder for additional agents. The Aspis remain unsure how to proceed. While she waits for a reply, Hamsa has ingratiated herself with the new count, Lethar Narsus, and now lives in the closest thing to luxury the muddy colony offers.

The Mireborn begin their ritual, darkening the skies even as a new ship of colonists arrives to reinforce Pridon's Hearth. Prematurely flush with victory, the lizardfolk have dispatched Daruthek's apprentice, the unstable druid Reszavass, to raid the human fortification called Fort Breakthrough for additional weapons and supplies, and to ambush anyone in Pridon's Hearth who stands a chance of halting their apocalyptic magic.

Weather

Weather plays an important role in this adventure, as a hurricane unnaturally builds off the coast and slowly moves ashore, impacting exploration and other outdoor activities. The weather changes as the PCs gain levels, or when the GM feels an increase is dramatically appropriate, giving the adventure a natural progression of tension as the PCs grow in power and come closer to stopping the Mireborn's ritual.

Off-Coast Storms (Level 1): As the adventure begins, the storms resulting from the Mireborn ritual are just forming off the western coast near Pridon's Hearth. The occasional rain cloud comes ashore, bringing a brief shower, but otherwise there is no impact on the PCs.

Vestigial Storms (Level 2): The larger storms have not yet struck the coast, but smaller storms begin making landfall. Pridon's Hearth and the surrounding region are engulfed in constant drizzle and rain, as well as light winds. Visibility ranges are reduced by one-quarter, and creatures take a –2 penalty on all Perception checks while outdoors.

Harbinger Storms (Level 3–4): The hurricane's arms begin to batter the coast. Heavy rains fall constantly, and severe winds buffet the land. There is a 25% chance each day that a thunderstorm forms over the region and lasts for the next 2d12 hours. The effects of rain, severe winds, and thunderstorms are further described on page 439 of the *Pathfinder RPG Core Rulebook*.

Landfall (Level 5+): The hurricane makes landfall, blanketing the region in rain, hurricane-force winds, and blown debris. Every day, there is a 50% chance that a tornado touches down within sight of the PCs, devastating a stretch of the marshlands (or Pridon's Hearth, at the GM's discretion).

Getting Started

As *Ire of the Storm* begins, the PCs are on their way to the Sargavan settlement of Pridon's Hearth. This adventure assumes the PCs have never been to Pridon's Hearth, and have heard only vague news about it in major Sargavan settlements such as Eleder, or from recruiters throughout the Inner Sea region. Many of the adventure's encounters involve getting to know the colony's unique and colorful inhabitants, and this works best if the PCs have little or no prior connection to Pridon's Hearth. Luckily, Count Narsus's call for a second wave of colonization reached beyond Sargava to the major cities of the Inner Sea region, making almost any sort of character concept or origin appropriate for this adventure.

The *Kaava Cutter*, a naval vessel that regularly runs cargo and passengers between Eleder and Port Freedom, makes monthly stops in Pridon's Hearth and serves as transport for the PCs. The passengers disembark the ship via smaller lifeboats, thanks to the town's lack of a proper dock. The adventure's first encounter assumes the PCs arrive via this ship, though it serves primarily to bring them to the attention of Sheriff Adaela and doesn't play any major role in the remainder of the adventure.

The GM may wish to begin this adventure on board the *Kaava Cutter*, giving the PCs some time to meet one another and flesh out their personalities and goals. GMs can also use this time to introduce the PCs to the assorted colonists making their way to Pridon's Hearth or foreshadow the Aspis presence via Mr. Blackwell (see the sidebar on page 6).

A RUDE WELCOME (CR 1)

Pridon's Hearth lacks a proper dock to accept large ships, so the PCs and other passengers arrive on a rotating batch of longboats on the smaller docks at Island Town. Gallio Menius (see the sidebar) demands to be the first ashore. The PCs and others arrive shortly thereafter. By the time the PCs' longboat arrives at the dock, Gallio is in the midst of directing his indentured laborers to organize belongings and farming supplies.

As the PCs disembark and collect their belongings on the fishing dock, an argument grows louder and louder between Gallio and a grizzled-looking man swaying at the end of the dock. The stranger is a local named Theos Votto, a carpenter who lost everything after coming to Pridon's Hearth when his wife and son died from malaria. Now drunk and bitter, he resents any newcomers, whom he regards as parasites coming to steal his livelihood. He's currently shouting for Gallio to leave the town, and the portly noble has no idea how to react to his hostile treatment. The drunken man delivers a punch that drives Gallio to the ground—wounding the noble's pride more than his body. Read or paraphrase the following.

"You should be getting out of this land, ya filthy leech!"

The drunk swings with a right hook and knocks Gallio to the deck planks, looking more shocked than injured. The swaying man ends his tirade by smashing the bottle he holds against a sturdy dock pylon. The bottle shatters, leaving him holding a vicious spike of serrated glass.

"And if yer not gonna leave... then I guess it's up to me to make ya!"

A successful DC 15 Perception or Sense Motive check reveals that Theos is intoxicated. Unless the PCs intervene within the next 3 rounds, he advances on Gallio, attacking the noble with his improvised dagger.

Creature: Unable to cope with the loss of his wife and son, Theos Votto loses hours or days to drunken fugues. His current stupor brought him to the docks today. He is hostile to the PCs and any other newcomer to Pridon's Hearth, so a successful DC 24 Diplomacy check is required to dissuade him from violence. His inebriated state makes him more emotional, granting the PCs a +5 circumstance bonus on Diplomacy checks. Alternatively, a successful DC 14 Intimidate check cows him but does nothing to improve his attitude. If any of the PCs attempt to approach Theos, or use less diplomatic means to subdue him, he wildly swings his shattered bottle and initiates combat.

THEOS VOTTO	CR 1

XP 400
Male human commoner 2/warrior 1
CN Medium humanoid (human)
Init +0; **Senses** Perception +4

DEFENSE

AC 11, touch 10, flat-footed 11 (+1 armor)
hp 18 (3 HD; 2d6+1d10+5)
Fort +3, **Ref** +2, **Will** +0

OFFENSE

Speed 30 ft.
Melee broken bottle +4 (1d4+2)

TACTICS

During Combat Theos swings his bottle at anyone who comes close. If one PC particularly agitates him, he attacks

that target, but is quick to change his mind and randomly attack others.

Morale Once reduced to fewer than 10 hit points, Theos surrenders by dropping his glass shard and falling to the ground, sobbing about his son and wife.

STATISTICS

Str 15, **Dex** 11, **Con** 12, **Int** 9, **Wis** 10, **Cha** 8

Base Atk +2; **CMB** +4; **CMD** 14

Feats Catch Off-Guard, Endurance, Lightning Reflexes

Skills Craft (carpentry) +4, Intimidate +4, Perception +4, Swim +6

Languages Common

Gear padded armor, broken bottle, 11 gp

Development: If the PCs manage to defuse the situation without violence, Theos wanders back to his home. Otherwise, the PCs need to subdue the raving drunk. Soon after the scuffle, Sheriff **Adaela Praet** (LN female human ex-paladin of Iomedae 3)—a serious but kind woman and the military commander of Pridon's Hearth—arrives with two members of the local militia. If Theos is still alive, the militia members cart the drunk off to a cell where he can sober up. Adaela is incensed if the PCs killed the carpenter, and she is particularly unnerved that their first act in town is murder. In this awkward scenario, Gallio vouches that the PCs defended him from Theos's murderous intentions, and offers to pay whatever fines are necessary to put the unpleasantness behind them.

As long as the PCs acted civilly, Sheriff Adaela introduces herself on behalf of the currently absent Count Narsus. She apologizes for not arriving earlier to prevent Theos's outburst, attributing her tardiness to being overworked and understaffed. She directs the newcomers to the Stone Hall or any of the local homes that take in lodgers, and allows them a night to settle in.

Story Award: In the PCs resolve the encounter nonviolently, award them XP as if they defeated Theos in combat.

The Break-In at Breakthrough

Once she has taken stock of all the colony's new arrivals and given them a night to rest, Sheriff Adaela sends word that she would like to meet with the PCs at the Stone Hall. If the PCs conducted themselves with decorum or fought Theos mercifully, she considers them the most trustworthy of Pridon's Hearth's new residents. If the PCs instead killed Theos, she would rather move their destructive impulses outside city limits as soon as possible. The sheriff pays for a few drinks and a hearty breakfast of eggs, roasted dika seeds, and fried taro; during the meal, she makes pleasantries for several minutes, hoping to take the PCs' measure.

Adaela offers little information about her personal background, stating only that she came from the distant town of Freehold in central Sargava. Tattoos on her arms bear the symbol of a sword and sunburst. A PC who succeeds at a DC 11 Knowledge (religion) check identifies this as the holy symbol of Iomedae, goddess of honor and justice. If questioned about it, Adaela rolls down her sleeves, brushing off her devotion as being "something from a long time ago."

After exchanging pleasantries, the sheriff explains her problem: Pridon's Hearth is an insular community that has had little contact with the region just outside its borders, with the exception of some adjacent farmlands. The colony maintains a single, small fort to the south to watch for potential problems. Fort Breakthrough hasn't sent a report in nearly 2 weeks—this isn't unheard of for the poorly organized military presence, but the sheriff is still concerned. Normally, the fort's personnel eagerly jump at the opportunity to return to civilization, if only for a single day.

Adaela wants to dispatch a small team, in case there has been any trouble. With her militia already understaffed, though, she can't spare even a single recruit. The new wave of settlers offers her a pool of potential new agents to travel 12 miles south to investigate the fort and report back. If the PCs agree, she offers them 100 gp up front to cover any equipment or expenses, and 50 gp each upon their return. If the PCs hold out for better rewards, Adaela has no more coin to offer, but a successful DC 16 Diplomacy check convinces her to cover their inn rooms for the foreseeable future.

Story Award: PCs who accept Adaela's offer earn 600 XP as well as directions to the nearby fort.

Around Pridon's Hearth

Sheriff Adaela suggests the PCs investigate the town a little before setting out for Fort Breakthrough. Talking to locals may teach them about the hazards they could face in the marsh and ensure they're properly equipped for their journey. She personally suggests the PCs visit Heri's Conservatorium, Northwind Smithy, and the Oyin Emporium before setting out, and possibly speaking with longtime residents around the Stone Hall. If the PCs ask about their advance, she provides them with a note of credit they can redeem at the Countinghouse of Abadar near the town gates.

Each of the following locations is detailed further in the Pridon's Hearth gazetteer on page 58.

Countinghouse of Abadar: The primary temple for Pridon's Hearth also serves as its bank and urban

ADAELA PRAET

INTRODUCTION

CHAPTER 1:
THE DELUGE

CHAPTER 2:
BEYOND THE COLONY

CHAPTER 3:
THE SKY TEMPEST TEMPLE

APPENDIX 1:
PRIDON'S HEARTH

APPENDIX 2:
BESTIARY

planning office, and any notes of credit the PCs receive during the adventure can be redeemed here for face value. Banker **Baldra Sifreth** (LN female venerable human cleric of Abadar 7) also encourages them to open accounts with the temple to protect their assets and invest in the community's future.

Banker Baldra apologizes for her slow pace as she fetches money or paperwork the PCs request. She normally relies on younger, part-time acolytes, but her assistant for that week—Quinn Vanicus—hasn't returned from her tour of duty at Fort Breakthrough. If the PCs mention they intend to visit the outpost, Baldra offers them 20 gp to check in on the young woman, and will double this reward if they escort her home safely or—should the worst have happened—bring her body back for a proper funeral. She feels responsible for her various acolytes and can't stand the idea of a loyal servant of Abadar being left alone in the untamed reaches.

Heri's Conservatorium: Run by the addled halfling **Heri Lightstep** (CN female halfling expert 3/alchemist[APG] 1), the apothecary sells potions, poultices, and a number of recreational compounds that are illegal in Sargava proper—and even Heri's non-recreational potions often come with side effects (see page 60).

Heri counts on several garrisoned troops at Fort Breakthrough to bring her specific jungle plants when they return with each weekly report. Short on supplies, she can offer only three *potions of cure light wounds* and a few alchemical remedies and weapons. If she learns of the PCs' expedition, she scribbles out a short list and says, "If you could keep an eyeball open for these, I'd appreciate it muchly." She promises an amazing reward if they bring her back usable samples. The adventurers can gather most of the supplies with a successful DC 20 Survival or Knowledge (nature) check, which requires an hour of foraging in the wilderness around the fort, or they can simply recover the bundle addressed to Heri in area **A9**. If the PCs bring back the halfling's supplies, she has forgotten she dispatched them, but eventually digs around through her stocks and rewards them with one *potion of lesser restoration* each from her personal stash (normally reserved to help her recover from bad drug trips).

Northwind Smithy: Vethorn Valgardson (N male half-elf expert 3/fighter 1) was one of the first newcomers from the second wave of settlement pushed by Count Narsus, and has lived in Pridon's Hearth only for the past year. He was born in the distant Lands of the Linnorm Kings, where he found himself somewhat ostracized for his elven heritage. He appreciates the general solitude and acceptance of the people of Pridon's Hearth, and enjoys the warmth here far more than his chilly native lands. Vethorn stocks all simple and martial weapons, and carries any light and medium metal armor. He can craft exotic weapons or heavy armor by request, requiring 1 day for every 20 gp of the item's market cost.

Vethorn spends most of his time crafting arms and armor for the local militia and paranoid residents, and if he realizes the PCs are headed for Fort Breakthrough, he asks them to check on a shipment he sent last month but for which he never received payment. If the PCs will bring back either his payment (95 gp) or the shipment (10 swords and 144 crossbow bolts), he promises them a 10% discount on all future purchases.

Oyin Emporium: The emporium stocks most of the nonmagical supplies available in Pridon's Hearth, and also serves as the local post office. **Mirya Oyin** (NG female old human expert 4) runs the shop, trading gossip and quips with customers and berating her deceased wife Cassia for passing on first and leaving the store in such a state of disarray. Her age makes walking difficult, so Mirya depends on locals to run a lot of her errands. If the PCs seem trustworthy (or can weather a few barbs), she asks them to deliver a parcel to the Witterwil farmstead a mile south of town on their way to the fort. She offers to loan them her *handy haversack* to hold all the farm supplies and seed, which they can continue to use afterward as long as they agree to perform the occasional delivery.

Story Award: Award the PCs 200 XP for each of the NPCs above that they meet.

A. FORT BREAKTHROUGH

This Sargavan advance outpost lies roughly 12 miles southeast of Pridon's Hearth—about 3 hours away when traveling via the muddy trail that connects it to town. The Witterwil farmstead lies between the two, and the human farmers there can offer the PCs a place to rest if they set out too late to reach the fort before nightfall.

The fort is a simple square structure, walled in with rough logs and perched on a short hill overlooking the nearby marshlands and coastline. Two-story towers anchor each corner of the fort, connected by wooden ramparts. Three stout, wooden buildings stand within the interior perimeter of the fort, two of them connected to the westernmost towers. See page 10 for a map for this location.

Fort Breakthrough housed eight militia members at a time from nearby Pridon's Hearth. A group of Song'o halflings—natives of the nearby Laughing Jungle—arrived at the fort just over a week ago, pleading for shelter from a raiding force that had attacked them. Only hours later, Mireborn lizardfolk, under the command of a fanatic named Reszavass, breached the main gate using a dinosaur as a battering ram. Reszavass executed the fort's messenger—an acolyte of Abadar named Quinn Vanicus—and crudely planted clues to make it appear as though the Song'o raided the structure.

Only a single witness survived the slaughter: the Song'o Muhdzuzi. Muhdzuzi hid in a storeroom (area **A11**) during the attack, and a collapsing beam sealed his hiding space, where he has remained for over a week, surviving on hardtack and rainwater that seeped through the leaky walls.

A1. Shattered Gate (CR 1)

The shattered remains of a heavy wooden door lie strewn across this opening in the log walls. Several of the flinders are trampled into the dirt. Some pieces of wood still remain attached to large metal hinges at the sides of the exposed entrance.

This was once the fort's main gate. Reszavass and her raiders guided a pachycephalosaurus to smash through the gate, leaving the dazed dinosaur to wander off—and clearing the path for the lizardfolk to overrun the fort's defenders.

Trap: The lizardfolk jury-rigged a trap from the debris of the gate to maim any militia members Pridon's Hearth dispatched to investigate. Passing through the gate might dislodge a heavy beam set overhead, but the trap's construction was rushed—any creature passing through the gate has only a 25% chance of triggering the trap.

FALLING BEAM TRAP	CR 1
Type mechanical; **Perception** DC 20; **Disable Device** DC 20	

EFFECTS

Trigger location; **Reset** none

Effect Atk +10 melee (2d4 bludgeoning damage); multiple targets (all targets in a 10-ft. square)

A2. Courtyard (CR 2)

Across this wide, muddy courtyard, three buildings cling to the sides of the fort's interior walls. Those to the southwest and the east are sealed tight, while the door to the building in the northwest is slightly ajar. A well squats near the northeastern end of the courtyard, while a fence between the southwestern and northwestern buildings forms a simple animal pen. Two human bodies—quickly decaying in the tropical sun—lie in the mud, one with a spear poking out from its chest.

Unprepared for the Mireborn's attack, the fort's militia never had the chance to react. The door to area **A5** is locked (Disable Device DC 25), and the door to area **A6** is blocked from the other side, requiring a successful DC 20 Strength check to force open. The door to area **A7** is ominously ajar.

Creatures: The shattering of the gateway left the fort open to animals. A trio of compsognathus dinosaurs made their way into the courtyard to snack on the dead humans and animals. The dinosaurs strike as soon as an intruder appears, fiercely defending their food supply. All three move to attack a single target at a time.

If PCs make a lot of noise in this courtyard, they may alert Zooif in area **A14**. With a successful DC 25 Perception check, the grippli notices any casual investigations (the DC is reduced to 20 if combat begins, or DC 10 if the PCs use any especially loud techniques, such as thunderstones). If she notices intruders, Zooif moves out to the parapets (area **A13**) and begins sniping at the humans 3 rounds later, croaking at them in Grippli to leave her new home.

COMPSOGNATHUSES (3)	CR 1/2

XP 200 each

hp 6 each (*Pathfinder RPG Bestiary 2* 90)

Development: Examining the two bodies found here may yield clues. With a successful DC 11 Knowledge (local) check, a PC identifies the spear as a hunting spear from one of the local Song'o halfling tribes. Both bodies have been gnawed by scavengers, but a successful DC 17 Heal check reveals that the Song'o spear was stabbed into one of the bodies after the man died. The second body is that of Quinn Vanicus, the missing acolyte from the Pridon's Hearth temple, who still wears her holy symbol of Abadar.

Story Award: If PCs return Quinn's body to the temple, award them 800 XP in addition to the priest's monetary reward (see page 8).

A3. Animal Pen

The mutilated carcasses of a half-dozen animals litter this pen. Bite and claw marks edge a section of the fence that has been shorn away, while the shoulder-high gate remains shut.

COMPSOGNATHUS

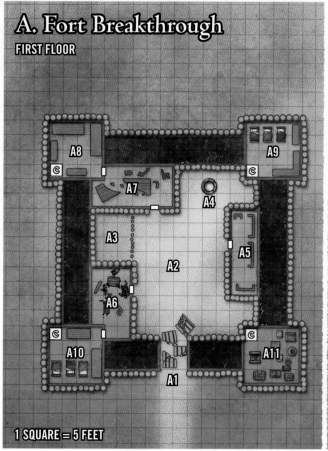

A. Fort Breakthrough
FIRST FLOOR

A8
A9
A7
A4
A3
A5
A2
A6
A10
A11
A1

1 SQUARE = 5 FEET

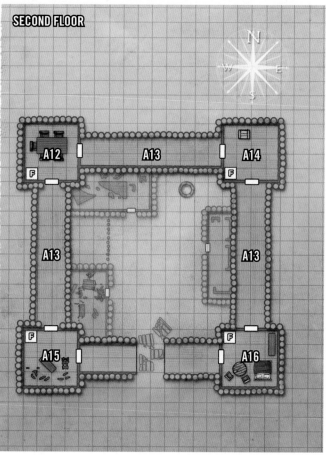

SECOND FLOOR

A12
A13
A14
A13
A13
A15
A16

Two goats and four pigs were once penned here, but now lie slain. The Mireborn made quick snacks of the animals while their leader investigated the interior of the fort.

Development: A successful DC 15 Heal check reveals the fatal injuries were caused by claw wounds, roughly the size of a humanoid hand, and that the most useful chunks of meat were cut free with a knife. Bites from the dinosaurs roaming the courtyard are more recent.

A4. Well

A sturdy stone well sits before the northernmost wall of the fort. An empty bucket hangs from a pulley over the dark shaft. A well-used dagger is embedded in the waterlogged bucket.

The well descends 30 feet, and is large enough to climb down. The dagger is a red herring left behind by Reszavass; with a successful DC 12 Knowledge (local) check, a PC identifies it as a Song'o blade.

Treasure: The dagger is a masterwork Small dagger. A PC who climbs down the well with a successful DC 10 Climb check finds 32 gp and a torn bandolier containing two cracked potion vials and a single intact *potion of cure light wounds*, along with a masterwork terbutje[UE] dropped by one of the lizardfolk invaders.

A5. Armory

This room has a single door. Wood-and-metal racks—their hinges slightly corroded from the tropical humidity—line the walls, each fitted with an assortment of arms and armor.

Fort Breakthrough's defenders never made it to their armory, cut off by the surprise and speed of the Mireborn attack. The only door into the armory is locked (Disable Device DC 25); a key from the fort commander's corpse in area **A16** is needed to open it.

Treasure: The armory contains five short swords, three longswords, four light crossbows, two heavy crossbows, 60 bolts, four suits of leather armor, two suits of studded leather armor, four heavy wooden shields, and a masterwork breastplate. A crate in the corner is packed with straw and contains an additional four short swords, four longswords, and 144 crossbow bolts—the most recent shipment delivered to the fort by Northwind Smithy.

Story Award: If the PCs return Vethorn's shipment or pay him the 95 gp owed for the crate (see page 8), award them an additional 800 XP. Vethorn won't buy his own goods off the PCs if he doesn't receive payment, and feels cheated if they keep the weapons or sell them to anyone else without paying him. If the PCs do either, he refuses to do business with them in the future.

INTRODUCTION

CHAPTER 1:
THE DELUGE

CHAPTER 2:
BEYOND THE COLONY

CHAPTER 3:
THE SKY TEMPEST TEMPLE

APPENDIX 1:
PRIDON'S HEARTH

APPENDIX 2:
BESTIARY

A6. Training Room

The eastern door of this wooden chamber is caved in, collapsing a makeshift barricade of haphazardly stacked shelves and crates. Three headless human bodies are impaled on the cabinets by crude spears. Flies buzz around the corpses, constantly landing on the crimson morass of gore where the heads were removed.

The soldiers of Fort Breakthrough were neither dedicated nor disciplined, and so they rarely used this larger room for anything more than naps and games of chance. The final few surviving soldiers of Fort Breakthrough made their last stand in the training room. Barricading the eastern entrance, they waited for the Mireborn to attack.

Treasure: The fort was under constant improvement, and one corner contains a chest of construction supplies—nails, rope, pulleys, hammers, saws, and chains, all of excellent quality. The crate is worth 150 gp and weighs 50 pounds, but may have other uses later in the chapter (see the sidebar on page 16).

Development: The bodies are heavily decayed, making the cause of death difficult to determine, but a successful DC 15 Heal check reveals that the spear thrusts occurred after death. With a successful DC 17 Perception check, a PC also finds a scaly, green hand in one corner, severed by one of the militia members during the final fight.

A7. Mess Hall

Broken halves of a large table lie askew in the center of this room. Half a dozen four-foot-long spears protrude from one half of the table, and brown bloodstains mar the floor. A basic map of the region covers most of one wall, hanging next to a picture of an austere-looking man.

When the Mireborn attackers broke down the fort's gate and charged inside, the militia rushed down to the courtyard, only to run directly into the advancing Mireborn warriors. After a brief struggle, they retreated into this hall, trying to link up with the rest of their scattered unit.

The large map depicts the coastline and rivers in great detail, but labels little else beyond the fort and Pridon's Hearth. GMs may wish to reveal the Korir River Delta poster map, included in this volume, to their players at this point. The portrait depicts Baron Utilinus, Grand Custodian of Sargava, who is identifiable with a successful DC 14 Knowledge (local) or Knowledge (nobility) check.

Treasure: The spears embedded in the table are all Song'o, and are identifiable as such with a successful DC 11 Knowledge (local) check. A successful DC 14 Perception check reveals a hidden cache behind the portrait of Baron Utilinus, containing 100 gp as part of the fort's payroll.

A8. Kitchen (CR 1)

Shelves bedeck the walls of this square room. A solid stone slab sits atop a waist-high counter at the northern edge of the room, covered with spoiled vegetables and rotting hunks of meat. A wooden door exits to the east, while a wooden ladder ascends fifteen feet to a second floor.

The fort's basic kitchen saw little violence. Fruits and vegetables are spoiled, but the westernmost pantry is closed.

Creatures: The fort suffered constantly from burrowing pests. An infestation of chaparral centipedes—a 3-foot-long breed of jungle vermin—plagued the fort's kitchen long before the Mireborn appeared. Four of these vermin lair in the kitchen; two are inside the westernmost cupboard, and the other two lurk under the baseboards. If the PCs spend any time exploring this chamber or open the cupboards, the centipedes attack. The two underground vermin break through the decayed floor boards as a move action, emerging in adjacent rooms if they need additional space.

CHAPARRAL CENTIPEDES (4)	CR 1/4

XP 100 each

N Small vermin

Init +3; **Senses** darkvision 60 ft.; Perception +4

DEFENSE

AC 13, touch 13, flat-footed 11 (+2 Dex, +1 size)

hp 3 (1d8–1)

Fort +1, **Ref** +2, **Will** +0

Immune mind-affecting effects

OFFENSE

Speed 30 ft., burrow 20 ft., climb 20 ft.

Melee bite +3 (1d3–3 plus poison)

Special Attacks poison

STATISTICS

Str 5, **Dex** 15, **Con** 8, **Int** —, **Wis** 10, **Cha** 2

Base Atk +0; **CMB** –4; **CMD** 8

Feats Weapon Finesse^B

Skills Acrobatics +2, Climb +11, Perception +4, Stealth +14;
   Racial Modifiers +4 Perception, +8 Stealth

SPECIAL ABILITIES

Poison (Ex) Bite—injury; *save* Fort DC 11; *frequency* 1/round for 6 rounds; *effect* 1d2 Dex damage; *cure* 1 save. The save DC is Constitution-based and includes a +2 bonus.

Treasure: The Mireborn grabbed anything of obvious value, including the soldiers' weapons, but ignored the fort's medical kit in the corner. The wooden trunk contains a healer's kit, two bottles of antiplague^{UE}, two bottles of antitoxin, four bottles of bloodblock^{UE}, and two sunrods, as well as bandages, wood alcohol, needles, thread, splints, and herbal tinctures worth a total of 100 gp. The medical kit may have other uses later in the chapter (see the sidebar on page 16).

A9. North Quarters

Three beds lie along most of the northern wall of this wooden chamber. A large wooden trunk along the eastern wall is opened, exposing haphazardly tossed clothing. The odor of spoiled meat wafts out from under the clothing. A cabinet runs across the southeastern walls, and a ladder ascends fifteen feet to the only exit.

Difficult to reach, this room was considered the worse of the fort's two personal quarters. Two of the three inhabitants made it out of the quarters to join the fight, while the third tried to don his armor and was caught unprepared by the invaders. Reszavass ordered the body to be hidden in the trunk and hastily covered, hoping it would be missed.

Treasure: Even a cursory search of the room uncovers a large, fragrant package of dried and pressed jungle plants with a note saying, "Quinn, please drop these off with Heri. Make sure she pays you up front for them, and tell her I'll have more red fern soon!"

Development: The body in the trunk has been maimed with claw marks and a chunk of its shoulder is missing—the result of a particularly enraged lizardfolk. Unlike the other bodies the PCs have found, no attempt has been made to conceal the cause of this man's death, and the clothes piled on top of the corpse have kept it from scavengers, giving PCs pristine evidence of the attackers' true nature.

Story Award: If the PCs deliver the package of herbs to Heri, award them an extra 800 XP in addition to the halfling's promised reward (see page 8).

A10. South Quarters

A trio of beds rest against the southern wall of the room, one concealing a lumpy, bloodstained mass within its blankets. A sturdy trunk lies against the northern wall, while an open cabinet stands to the east. A ladder in the northwestern corner leads to the floor above, while a shoddy door exits to the northeast. Drops of blood mark a trail from the ladder to the beds, and three more spears lie on the floor.

Once she finished the slaughter, Reszavass claimed the heads of her opponents and left this corpse in a bed.

Development: The corpse here shows fewer signs of violence, beyond the missing head. A successful DC 15 Heal check reveals that the head was removed after death, and succeeding at this check by 5 or more also reveals the frostbite—unusual in the region's tropical climate—resulting from Reszavass's magic.

A11. Storage (CR 1/2)

Boxes and barrels line the sides of this dark, wooden room. A ladder ascends to a trap door, fifteen feet above.

Dry goods, nails, canvas, fresh clothing, and other basic supplies were kept in this chamber, located under the former fort commander's quarters for security.

Creature: The single survivor of the fort massacre, a Song'o halfling named Muhdzuzi, hid from the Mireborn during the attack, only to be trapped when a bookcase above toppled and sealed the trap door. After a week of isolation and little water, he is desperate but extremely wary of strangers—Song'o are generally isolationist, and the violence of the assault has left deep psychological scars on the hunter's psyche. He also fears the grippli Zooif (see area **A14**), who claims the areas above, and remains as quiet as possible at all times to avoid alerting her to his presence.

Muhdzuzi is dehydrated and suffers from the fatigued condition. He speaks only Halfling and Polyglot, though a PC who succeeds at a DC 15 Linguistics check can decipher and convey basic concepts.

After his ordeal, Muhdzuzi has a starting attitude of unfriendly toward any strangers, and he shouts threats while swinging his dagger wildly at anyone who draws near. With a successful DC 20 Diplomacy check, a PC can calm the halfling; characters who speak Halfling or offer him water gain a +5 circumstance bonus on this check.

MUHDZUZI	CR 1/2

XP 200
Male halfling expert 1/warrior 1
N Small humanoid (halfling)
Init +1; **Senses** Perception +2

DEFENSE

AC 15, touch 12, flat-footed 14 (+3 armor, +1 Dex, +1 size)
hp 13 (2 HD; 1d8+1d10+3)
Fort +4, **Ref** +2, **Will** +3; +2 vs. fear

OFFENSE

Speed 25 ft.
Melee dagger +2 (1d3/19–20)
Ranged sling +3 (1d3)

TACTICS

During Combat Muhdzuzi fears outsiders after his ordeal. If the PCs don't establish communication or calm him within 3 rounds, he attacks, hoping to drive the PCs away long enough to escape.

Morale Muhdzuzi hopes to flee rather than die fighting, and makes a break for the ladder as soon as it seems clear.

MUHDZUZI

INTRODUCTION

CHAPTER 1:
THE DELUGE

CHAPTER 2:
BEYOND THE COLONY

CHAPTER 3:
THE SKY TEMPEST TEMPLE

APPENDIX 1:
PRIDON'S HEARTH

APPENDIX 2:
BESTIARY

STATISTICS

Str 11, **Dex** 13, **Con** 12, **Int** 9, **Wis** 10, **Cha** 10

Base Atk +1; **CMB** +0; **CMD** 11

Feats Fleet

Skills Acrobatics +2 (–2 when jumping), Climb +5, Knowledge (nature) +3, Perception +2, Profession (trapper) +4, Stealth +8, Survival +5; **Racial Modifiers** +2 Acrobatics, +2 Climb, +2 Perception

Languages Halfling, Polyglot

Gear wooden armor^UE, dagger, sling with 10 bullets, animal snares, Song'o necklace (worth 15 gp)

Treasure: Although Muhdzuzi nibbled on the contents of the large crate of rations here, it still contains 100 gp worth of food, which may have other uses later in the chapter (see the sidebar on page 16).

Development: If any PCs speak Halfling or Polyglot, once calmed, Muhdzuzi shares everything he saw regarding the Mireborn's assault on the fort. He and six other hunters encountered the raiding party 9 days ago and fled toward the coast, only to discover the human fort. Setting aside their traditional isolationism, the Song'o asked the strangers for shelter from the lizardfolk. Sadly, none of the resident soldiers could understand the halflings, and their warnings went unheard until the Mireborn attacked that night. Muhdzuzi would like to return to his village, Cahshil, to the north, but he is afraid to travel alone and remains with the PCs unless chased away or given shelter somewhere safe (like Pridon's Hearth).

Story Award: If the PCs manage to calm Muhdzuzi and hear his account of what happened, award them an additional 800 XP.

A12. Strategy Room

A long wooden table covered in scattered paperwork fills much of this room. A decapitated human corpse is slumped across the mess. Doors exit the room to the south and east, while a ladder in the southwestern corner descends to the first floor of the fort.

The body on the table is yet another militia member, slower to flee than her companions, who was slain and beheaded by Reszavass. The paperwork is all manner of mundane reports, describing local water sources, plants, animal migrations, and daily weather reports.

Development: The woman here bears puncture wounds, and a DC 12 Heal check confirms she was killed with a spear. Exceeding this DC by 5 or more reveals that all the wounds were delivered from above, as if she were stabbed by someone her height or taller. With a successful DC 18 Perception check, a PC finds a single footprint left in the victim's blood on a piece of scattered paperwork; the footprint is human-sized with clawed toes, and a PC who succeeds at a DC 15 Knowledge (local) or Survival check identifies the creature who made it as a lizardfolk.

A13. Parapets

A wooden walkway, raised fifteen feet above the ground, connects two towers of the fort. Thick logs form a makeshift barrier against the outside world, rising up two feet from the edge of the walkway.

These walkways line the outer wall of the fort, connecting the second-level towers. The height provides an unobstructed view of most of the courtyard while granting occupants cover from attacks outside the fort.

A14. Watchtower (CR 2)

Six wide arrow slits look out over the surrounding marshland. Straw is piled up in the corner of this chamber, opposite a single ladder that descends to a lower level. A lockbox rests beside the straw, with a pillow propped against it. Two doors exit to the west and south.

The tallest tower of the fort, this structure served as the lookout from which the militia kept watch over the area. Since the Mireborn raid, a squatter has moved in, using the tower as a hunting stand and makeshift sleeping area.

Creature: A grippli exile named Zooif settled in the delta area many years ago, and claimed this tower as her new home after she watched the Mireborn leave. The PCs find Zooif here if they haven't already gained her attention by being loud in the courtyard. Zooif shoots first and asks questions later; her starting attitude is hostile.

ZOOIF	CR 2

XP 600

Female grippli ranger 3 (*Pathfinder RPG Bestiary 2* 149)

CN Small humanoid (grippli)

Init +7; **Senses** darkvision 60 ft.; Perception +8

DEFENSE

AC 17, touch 14, flat-footed 14 (+3 armor, +3 Dex, +1 size)

hp 27 (3d10+6)

Fort +5, **Ref** +6, **Will** +3

OFFENSE

Speed 30 ft., climb 20 ft.

Melee mwk battleaxe +5 (1d6/×3) or net +4 (entangle)

Ranged mwk longbow +8 (1d6/×3)

Special Attacks combat style (archery), favored enemy (animals +2)

TACTICS

During Combat Zooif prefers a running fight, using her net and tanglefoot bag to slow down opponents. She uses Deadly Aim at all times. The grippli fears dogs and similar creatures far more than people, and targets animal companions first, but saves her magic arrows for bigger game.

Morale If reduced to fewer than 8 hit points, Zooif tries to flee the fort, using her *potion of pass without trace* to evade any pursuers. If she escapes, the PCs could encounter her again as they explore the area in Chapter 2.

Str 11, **Dex** 17, **Con** 14, **Int** 10, **Wis** 14, **Cha** 8

Base Atk +3; **CMB** +2; **CMD** 15

Feats Deadly Aim, Endurance, Improved Initiative, Point-Blank Shot

Skills Climb +12, Craft (bows) +5, Handle Animal +4, Heal +7, Knowledge (geography) +5, Knowledge (nature) +6, Perception +8, Stealth +12 (+16 in marshes and forested areas), Survival +8, Swim +4

Languages Grippli, Polyglot

SQ camouflage, favored terrain (jungle +2), swamp stride, track +1, wild empathy +2

Combat Gear *+1 animal-bane arrows* (3), *potions of cure light wounds* (2), *potion of pass without trace*, antitoxin, defoliant^UE, tanglefoot bag; **Other Gear** mwk studded leather, mwk battleaxe, mwk longbow, net, civet pelt (worth 15 gp), parrot feathers (27; worth 5 sp each)

Treasure: Zooif's lockbox contains the alchemical items and shiny objects she scavenged while looting the fort, but she closed the lid on the chest without realizing she didn't have a key. The chest is locked (Disable Device DC 30), and the only key is on the corpse of the fort commander in area **A16**. The chest contains 112 gp, a silver holy symbol of Erastil (25 gp), a silver flatware setting (20 gp as a set), three bottles of acid, two tanglefoot bags, and a thunderstone.

ZOOIF

Development: Should the PCs manage to negotiate with Zooif or subdue her in combat, the grippli begrudgingly discusses her past. Exiled from her tribe for causing the death of tadpoles, she now trades furs for alchemical items and potions with various colonial explorers. She came to Fort Breakthough to trade, only to witness lizardfolk from the Mireborn tribe departing the scene, carrying a half-dozen dead halflings with them. She rooted around for a few nice trinkets, and decided to camp out in the fort, which made an excellent hunting blind.

Zooif doesn't know or especially like the militia—she can't tell one human from another—but she bore them no ill will. She has trouble processing death or mourning others—which is in part why she ended up exiled from her tribe—and doesn't understand if anyone seems upset.

A15. Shrine (CR 2)

Two wooden doors to the east and north allow access to this square chamber. A single bench rests before a scene of destruction, with smashed pottery and broken statues dashed on the floor. Two child-sized corpses rest amid the detritus, peppered with arrows, and with blood smeared on the floor and debris around them.

The fort's shrine contained simple clay statues of assorted gods. Reszavass smashed the "false idols" in these chambers, and killed two of the Song'o they found hiding within, then stabbed them with crossbow bolts from the militia's arsenal to further sell the image of a battle between the Song'o and the colonial forces.

Haunt: The desecration of the holy chamber and the brutal murder of the terrified halflings has spawned a haunt, hinting at the Mireborn's efforts to frame the Song'o. The haunt triggers if either of the corpses is disturbed.

SONG'O EXECUTION HAUNT	CR 2

XP 600

CN persistent haunt (20-ft.-by-20-ft. room)

Caster Level 2nd

Notice Perception DC 18 (hear random mutterings in Polyglot and notice the shattered holy icons shaking)

hp 9; **Weakness** tricked by *hide from undead*; **Trigger** proximity; **Reset** 1 day

Effect Once a body is disturbed, each person in the room is suddenly compelled to draw a crossbow bolt from one of the halfling bodies and stab himself in the torso with it, dealing a number of points of damage equal to 1d6 + his Strength modifier. This effect is similar to the spell *murderous command*^APG, but afflicted targets are compelled to harm themselves, reflecting the way the Song'o bodies were staged and then stabbed after the fact.

Destruction To destroy this haunt, the Song'o bodies must be returned to Cahshil and cremated by their people.

INTRODUCTION

CHAPTER 1:
THE DELUGE

CHAPTER 2:
BEYOND THE COLONY

CHAPTER 3:
THE SKY TEMPEST TEMPLE

APPENDIX 1:
PRIDON'S HEARTH

APPENDIX 2:
BESTIARY

Story Award: If the PCs return the Song'o bodies to their people for proper services, award them an additional 600 XP.

A16. Commander's Quarters (CR 3)

A bookshelf lies face down in the northwestern corner of this wooden room, partially concealing a trap door beneath. In the opposite corner is a large bed with a noticeable bump under its rumpled sheets. A small table with two chairs sits in the southwest corner. Doors exit to the north and west.

The Mireborn slew Marcus Pandellion, the fort's commander, in his room before he could respond to their invasion. The books here are primarily poetry and tales of adventure. Imported from Cheliax as entertainment for the militia members, they're already moldering from the humidity and are of no particular value. The lumpy mass on the bed is Commander Marcus Pandellion, one of Sheriff Adaela's oldest friends; atop his body lies a crude note written in Common (see Handout #1).

A trap door down to area **A11** is sealed by the fallen bookshelf. Muhdzuzi is desperate; if the PCs don't investigate the trap door themselves, he begins calling for help after a few minutes.

Creatures: The rotting body and open windows here attracted far more flies than anywhere else in the fort, and a large colony of spiders has moved in to prey on the buzzing masses, including an exceptionally big specimen of the jungle pests.

GIANT SPIDER	CR 1

XP 400

hp 16 (*Pathfinder RPG Bestiary* 258)

SPIDER SWARM	CR 1

XP 400

hp 9 (*Pathfinder RPG Bestiary* 258)

Treasure: The commander's corpse wears masterwork studded leather armor, has a masterwork silver dagger tucked in its boot, and possesses a pouch containing 126 sp and the keys to area **A5** and the chest in area **A14**.

Development: Pandellion's body is desiccated thanks to the giant spider, and hence less decomposed, but a successful DC 19 Heal or Perception check reveals an obsidian shard lodged in one of his ribs. The shard is too large to be a halfling spear point, and matches a piece missing from the terbutje in area **A4**.

If the PCs confront Muhdzuzi with the letter, he's puzzled and unable to read Common. Only his tribal leader, Zaahku, speaks the outsider language, and her hand is both smaller and steadier.

Story Award: If the PCs find the fort commander's body, award them an additional 800 XP.

WE NO LONGER LET HUMANS RUIN RIVER! LEAVE SONG'O LANDS, OR WE KILL AGAIN! -CAHSHIL TRIBE

Handout #1

Returning from Fort Breakthrough

Once the PCs complete their investigation of the fort, they have likely accumulated enough evidence to know the Song'o halflings were not the true perpetrators. If they saved Muhdzuzi, the PCs have a witness to describe the Mireborn presence—though the halfling can describe them only as lizardfolk, unaware of their specific affiliation. If the PCs did not save Muhdzuzi and remained ignorant of the various clues at the fort, it is possible they believe the Song'o performed the attack.

The weather begins to worsen once the PCs leave Fort Breakthrough; drizzle, light rain, and gusting winds begin buffeting the area as the first vestigial storm strikes the coast. Wandering animals desperately seek shelter from the coming storm, which the PCs should spot in the distance as they travel. A constant, gray haze covers the sky, darkening to an ominous black in the west.

Regardless of their findings and resulting beliefs, the PCs still need to return to Pridon's Hearth to present their information to Sheriff Adaela and complete whatever favors they agreed to undertake for the townsfolk. The folks of Pridon's Hearth pay their debts, but remain distracted by the sudden and dramatic change in the weather.

If the PCs bring Muhdzuzi back to town, Sheriff Adaela is skeptical of the halfling's story. She discounts his report as a wild tale to conceal his guilt in the fort massacre—as no one in Pridon's Hearth has ever seen the lizardfolk so far south, or so aggressive. If the PCs provide any additional evidence of the lizardfolk threat (such as the terbutje found in area **A4**, the severed hand found in area **A6**, or an expert analysis of the bodies), she changes her mind and accepts the halfling's account. If the PCs provide no evidence in Muhdzuzi's defense, the sheriff throws him into a holding cell until she can conduct a proper investigation.

Preparation Points

As the PCs rush to help Pridon's Hearth prepare for the encroaching storm, GMs can track their efforts using Preparation Points (PP). The number of Preparation Points the town accrues determines how effectively it weathers the squall, how quickly the citizens get back on their feet, and how many XP the heroes earn for their hard work.

The PCs can earn Preparation Points for the town by assisting in the town's readiness, by gathering citizens into safe locations, and by making donations to the collective good. If the PCs donate the crate of construction supplies from area **A6**, award the town an additional 2 Preparation Points. If they donate the medical supplies from area **A8**, award them an additional 2 Preparation Points. If they donate the rations from area **A11**, award them an additional 1 Preparation Point. At the GM's discretion, any other relevant actions performed by the PCs, such as donating valuable magic items or casting spells like *bless* to keep the community calm, should each be rewarded with an additional 1 Preparation Point.

PP Total	Results
5 or fewer	**Survival and Little Else**: Pridon's Hearth is devastated, with dozens of deaths. Many buildings are leveled or flooded. All shops are unavailable for a week, and once they reopen, prices are 50% higher than normal for 1d4 weeks. Reward the PCs with 600 XP for surviving.
6–12	**Battered but Standing**: Many of the town's cheaper buildings are lost causes, and will need to be rebuilt in coming months. All shops are closed for 3 days, after which there's a cumulative 25% chance each day a given business will reopen. Reward the PCs with 1,600 XP.
13–19	**Relatively Intact**: Broken windows and flooding damage a few homes. Businesses reopen within 2 days. Reward the PCs with 4,000 XP.
20+	**Cosmetic Damage**: The storm leaves little damage beyond mud and a few loose shingles. Shops reopen the same day, and the citizens of Pridon's Hearth offer the PCs a reward of 250 gp each. Award the PCs 5,600 XP for the party's extraordinary efforts.

Story Award: If the PCs discover the truth behind the attack or at least exonerate the Song'o halflings, award them 200 XP each.

The Storm Approaches

Within several hours of the PCs' return, the weather takes a swift turn for the worse as a powerful storm front breaks away from the growing mass offshore and begins barreling directly toward the tiny town. Sheriff Adaela coordinates the citizens, decreeing that the Stone Hall will serve as a temporary headquarters and as a refuge for evacuees—an unusually high storm tide already laps at the lowest streets of Island Town. Adaela sends a deputy to bring the PCs to her, hoping these extraordinary newcomers might throw in with the defense of their new home.

Adaela asks the PCs to help with numerous tasks, deputizing them as her agents and granting them the authority to issue commands on her behalf and arrest criminals. She overlooks offering payment, but if the PCs press the matter, she assures them they'll be rewarded—if there's a town left after the storm comes.

EVENT 1: HELPING AROUND TOWN

The PCs can assist the town's disaster preparations in a variety of ways. Sheriff Adaela summarizes several options that will help everyone weather the unexpected storm: reinforcing weaker structures, collecting supplies in sturdy shelters, and keeping the citizens calm and coordinated. This is an opportunity for the PCs to split up and showcase their best skills.

Each task presents a possible skill check, and the town earns 1 Preparation Point (see the sidebar) for each skill check at which a PC succeeds. If a PC exceeds the listed DC by 5 or more, her efforts are especially helpful and earn the town 2 Preparation Points instead. Each PC can attempt a check only once, but multiple PCs can attempt the same check. The PCs will be working alongside residents of Pridon's Hearth, and GMs can reward exceptional roleplaying with a +2 circumstance bonus on related skill checks to help secure the community. Four hours remain to prepare the town before the PCs must take shelter from the storm, and each skill check represents 2 hours of work, allowing each adventurer to attempt two skill checks.

- **Boarding Up**: The first goal is to board up any glass windows, shutters, or openings in buildings that rain and wind could break through, and secure any buildings that rely on canvas roofs or walls. The PCs can attempt the following skill checks: Craft (carpentry) or Profession (woodcutter) to cut properly sized boards, Climb to reach roofs and eaves, and Knowledge (engineering) or Profession (engineer) to identify structural weaknesses. The PCs can also attempt Strength or Wisdom checks to work efficiently and tirelessly. A PC who succeeds at a DC 12 check using any of these skills or abilities earns the town 1 Preparation Point.

- **Keeping the Peace**: Already an independent lot unaccustomed to cooperating, the people of Pridon's Hearth grow restless with the approaching storm. More vocal PCs can calm or even coordinate the townsfolk

into an effective unit. The PCs can attempt the following skill checks: Diplomacy to reason with townsfolk, Intimidate or Profession (soldier) to cow them into helping, Perform to keep people entertained and relieve stress, and Sense Motive to determine moods and assign the townsfolk tasks to keep them occupied. The PCs can also attempt Charisma or Intelligence checks to motivate people with charm or logic. A PC who succeeds at DC 12 check using any of these skills or abilities earns the town 1 Preparation Point.

- **Moving Supplies:** Food, water, clothing, and emergency supplies must be collected in secure locations, like the Stone Hall and the Countinghouse of Abadar. The PCs can attempt the following skill checks: Appraise or Profession (merchant) to determine the most useful medical supplies and foodstuffs, Handle Animal or Profession (driver) to coerce the town's few beasts of burden to haul goods, and Ride to better navigate the hazards created by the wind and rain. The PCs can also attempt Constitution or Dexterity checks to act as haulers, relying on endurance or speed instead of skill. A PC who succeeds at a DC 12 check using any of these skills or abilities earns the town 1 Preparation Point.

EVENT 2: TAKING ITS TROLL (CR 5)

This event can occur either as the PCs complete their initial storm preparations or after searching for Maso's missing cat in **Event 4** (see page 18).

Creature: Emboldened by the storm and growing chaos, a troll from the nearby jungle has come into town to loot the vacant buildings. Graular bashes open a few homes, stuffing odds and ends into her bag, before trying to break into the bakery. The PCs may hear the commotion of the troll's looting, or may be sent by Sheriff Adaela to confront the troll after several guards return to the Stone Hall injured.

Graular has already encountered a pack of torch-wielding guards, and is nearly fed up. Thanks to her regeneration, the PCs may not have the tools to defeat her permanently, but the troll's heart isn't in the looting anymore, and she attempts to flee back to her jungle lair with her bag of goodies if reduced to fewer than 25 hit points. She can also be bought off, agreeing to leave in exchange for 200 gp worth of shiny objects or weapons, or for the crate of rations the PCs may have retrieved from area **A11** of Fort Breakthrough. At the GM's discretion, if the troll flees, the PCs may encounter her again as they explore the surrounding area in Chapter 2.

GRAULAR   **CR 5**

XP 1,600

Female troll (*Pathfinder RPG Bestiary* 268)

hp 63

Melee club +8 (1d8+5), bite +6 (1d8+2), claw +6 (1d6+2)

Feats Intimidating Prowess, Iron Will, Multiattack

Treasure: Graular's looting spree hit several homes as well as a salvage office. Her bag contains a variety of nearly worthless plates, cutlery, paintings, and pillows, as well as two *potions of cure moderate wounds*, a *scroll of water breathing*, a *wand of touch of the sea*[APG] (3rd level, 15 charges remaining), and six amethyst gems worth 70 gp each.

Development: If the PCs fail to defeat or drive off Graular, she continues her looting spree for another half hour before returning to the jungle to find shelter, reducing the town's Preparation Point total by 3.

EVENT 3: THE STRAGGLERS

Sheriff Adaela appreciates the PCs' efforts in reinforcing the town. By now, the final preparations are in place, but several citizens refuse to abandon their homes in Island Town. Adaela knows of three specific individuals residing in Island Town who refuse to move, and she asks the PCs to convince them to retreat to the safety of the town proper. The sheriff provides the address for each.

Amal Rashid (LN male commoner 2) lived with his mother until she passed three summers ago. His refusal to depart his home stems from severe agoraphobia—a fear of crowds and open spaces—and the thought of living in the communal shelters on the mainland horrifies him. He welcomes the PCs into his home, though groups of more than two put him on edge. A successful DC 18 Sense Motive check reveals his phobia, giving PCs some insight into his apprehension. Convincing Amal to leave requires a successful DC 22 Diplomacy check or a successful DC 18 Intimidate check, and he offers the PCs a one-time bribe of 500 gp—his life savings, which he and his mother had planned to use to open a cobbler's shop—if they agree to leave him be. Alternatively, PCs can help reinforce the man's home against the oncoming storm, saving him from the panic-inducing crowds at the shelter. If the PCs convince him to leave, or succeed at a DC 12 Craft (carpentry) or Profession (engineer) check to reinforce Rashid's home, they earn the town 1 Preparation Point.

Maso Pareto (N male commoner 4) is eccentric even by local standards. Maso maintains a constantly growing stable of house cats from all across the Inner Sea. All but one of the cats has been safely transported to sturdier lodgings at the temple of Abadar, but when the PCs encounter Maso, he's outside calling for a last cat, Delour. Maso refuses to leave Island Town until the cat is safe, though a successful DC 14 Bluff or Diplomacy check convinces Maso to depart for shelter if the PCs agree to find Delour and bring him to safety. Maso offers the PCs the pearl on Delour's collar in exchange for the cat's return, in addition to vacating to the walled section of the city. Whether they agree to look for Delour or not, the cat shows up in the following storm event. If the PCs convince Maso to leave, they earn the town 1 Preparation Point.

Mirya Oyin (NG female old human expert 4)—the cantankerous owner of Oyin's Emporium—refuses to

INTRODUCTION

CHAPTER 1: THE DELUGE

CHAPTER 2: BEYOND THE COLONY

CHAPTER 3: THE SKY TEMPEST TEMPLE

APPENDIX 1: PRIDON'S HEARTH

APPENDIX 2: BESTIARY

abandon the store she and her late wife built together, fearing recent arrivals (possibly even the PCs) might loot the shop. Mirya constantly redirects the conversation, trying to sell the PCs random items in her shop or demanding to know why they haven't yet gone to safety. She also insists on dubbing the growing storm "Hurricane Cassia" in honor of her deceased wife—as "Only Cassia ever caused such a ruckus around here." Convincing Mirya to leave requires a successful DC 15 Diplomacy check or DC 20 Intimidate check; mentioning Cassia or agreeing to name the storm after Mirya's departed wife provides PCs a +2 circumstance bonus on Diplomacy checks. If the PCs convince Mirya to leave, they earn the town 1 Preparation Point.

MIRYA OYIN

EVENT 4: THAT DARNED CAT (CR 3)

This event occurs once the PCs finish dealing with the stragglers in the previous event and begin heading back to the mainland, or if they search for Maso's cat. The PCs hear the meows of a cat from the hastily erected barricades near the western edge of Island Town.

Creatures: Delour the cat, a particularly corpulent example of the feline species, crawled into an unused carriage to take a nap and find shelter from the rain, and the townsfolk didn't think to look inside before making the vehicle part of the barricades they built to keep water from flooding the nearby streets. Now awake, Delour howls for release from the closed carriage, the noise audible even over the gathering storm. When released, Delour plods along, oblivious to events around him, and spends his actions tugging at the pants of the PCs, despite the rain, begging for offerings of food.

Two tainted water elementals, by-products of the Mireborn's ritual tapping into the Elemental Planes, arrive in advance of the greater storm. Their bashing against the barricade—which they consider an insult to the freedom of water—originally woke Delour from his nap. They now push along the barricade from the riverside, steadily weakening it, while simultaneously searching for the source of the cat's howls. PCs opening the carriage to release Delour are targeted by the elementals, who leap over the barricade to attack.

The constant downpour from the approaching storm leaves each PC as standing in water for the purpose of the water elemental's water mastery ability.

DELOUR	CR 1/4

XP 100

Cat (*Pathfinder RPG Bestiary* 131)

hp 3

TAINTED WATER ELEMENTALS (2)	CR 1

XP 400 each

NE Small water elementals (*Pathfinder RPG Bestiary* 126)

hp 13 each

Treasure: Delour's collar contains a single pearl, a family heirloom Maso used to decorate his pet. The pearl is actually a *pearl of power* (1st level); this is the treasure Maso promised them if they agreed to find Delour.

Development: The PCs earn the XP for saving Maso Pareto (as listed in **Event 3**) by saving Delour. If the PCs fail to defeat the elementals, the creatures eventually break the barricades in several locations and the water seeps into much of the surrounding area; subtract 2 Preparation Points from the town's final total.

EVENT 5: THE MIREBORN STRIKE (CR 5)

This event coincides with the arrival of this first storm, and occurs after the PCs have completed all their preparations. As the storm makes landfall, successive cracks of thunder echo across the settlement. Anyone outdoors or watching through windows can plainly see these strikes all touching down around the northern barricades of Island Town. The strikes continue every few minutes, clearly indicating some unnatural force directing them. Sheriff Adaela departs to investigate, but fails to return even as the strikes become more frequent.

If the PCs don't move to investigate themselves, other figures in town ask them to do so, going so far as to mention that the good sheriff would be unable to pay them for their services to the community if she's dead.

Creatures: Atop Island Town's barricades stands Reszavass, a religious fanatic and leader of the Mireborn's raids. Her is belt is lined with the severed heads of the militia members of Fort Breakthrough, their faces pruned by water and contorted in horrified expressions. Reszavass's presence agitates the storm, bringing down lightning and increased rainfall—the result of her being one of the secondary casters who partook in the original casting of the storm summoning ritual. Three Mireborn raiders guard her, advancing on any creatures approaching the barricades and their leader. They attempt to block PCs from attacking Reszavass, and specifically target enemies casting spells or making ranged attacks when they can.

The raiders knocked Sheriff Adaela unconscious in their confrontation, but Reszavass decided such an important human would make an excellent trophy to present Daruthek after their raid, and has left her alive for now.

INTRODUCTION

CHAPTER 1:
THE DELUGE

CHAPTER 2:
BEYOND THE COLONY

CHAPTER 3:
THE SKY TEMPEST TEMPLE

APPENDIX 1:
PRIDON'S HEARTH

APPENDIX 2:
BESTIARY

RESZAVASS — CR 3

XP 800

Female lizardfolk druid 3 (*Pathfinder RPG Bestiary* 195)

NE Medium humanoid (reptilian)

Init +1; **Senses** Perception +6

DEFENSE

AC 18, touch 11, flat-footed 17 (+2 armor, +1 Dex, +5 natural)

hp 36 (5d8+13)

Fort +8, **Ref** +2, **Will** +7

OFFENSE

Speed 30 ft., swim 15 ft.

Melee bite +4 (1d4+1), 2 claws +4 (1d4+1)

Domain Spell-Like Abilities (CL 3rd; concentration +5)

5/day—lightning arc (1d6+1 electricity)

Druid Spells Prepared (CL 3rd; concentration +5)

2nd—*bear's endurance, chill metal* (DC 14), *wind wall*ᴰ

1st—*entangle* (DC 13), *hydraulic push*ᴬᴾᴳ, *magic fang, obscuring mist*ᴰ

0 (at will)—*create water, detect poison, purify food and drink* (DC 12), *resistance*

D Domain spell; **Domain** Air

TACTICS

Before Combat If Reszavass notices strangers approaching from her high perch, she casts *bear's endurance* on herself.

During Combat Reszavass remains above the fight, protecting herself with *wind wall* and using her *entangle, chill metal,* and lightning arcs to target enemies.

Morale Reszavass fights until the death, believing the power of the storm will protect her.

STATISTICS

Str 13, **Dex** 12, **Con** 15, **Int** 7, **Wis** 14, **Cha** 14

Base Atk +3; **CMB** +4; **CMD** 15

Feats Iron Will, Multiattack, Power Attack

Skills Acrobatics +5, Handle Animal +7, Knowledge (nature) +5, Perception +6, Survival +9, Swim +13; **Racial Modifiers** +4 Acrobatics

Languages Druidic, Polyglot

SQ hold breath, nature bond (Air domain), nature sense, trackless step, wild empathy +5, woodland stride

Combat Gear *brooch of shielding, wand of cure moderate wounds* (8 charges); **Other Gear** mwk leather armor

LIZARDFOLK (3) — CR 1

XP 400 each

hp 11 each (*Pathfinder RPG Bestiary* 195)

Development: If Reszavass falls in combat, the lightning strikes grow less frequent and less centralized, though the storm remains for several hours. If the PCs fail to defeat Reszavass, she and her followers finish destroying the barricades, flooding much of Island Town and reducing the town's Preparation Point total by 4. In addition, if left free, the lizardfolk raiders take Sheriff Adaela back with

them into the jungle, where she may need to be rescued later in the adventure, or she may be sacrificed to feed the forming hurricane, serving as a small example of what will come should the PCs fail to stop the Mireborn's plot.

Aftermath

The thunderstorm continues to rage throughout the night, but by morning it has subsided into a light drizzle. To the west, though, the growing hurricane remains plainly visible as it continues to gather mass. See the sidebar on page 16 to see how the town weathered the storm. If damage isn't too severe, the people of Pridon's Hearth thank the PCs for everything they have done so far, then begin more methodical preparations for the much bigger storm to come. Sheriff Adaela (if she's been rescued) encourages the heroes to get some rest, and assures them they will be compensated, as Count Narsus will soon be holding a meeting to discuss recent events.

Story Award: With the initial storm finally over, consult the Preparation Points sidebar on page 16 to determine how many bonus XP the heroes earned for their efforts. This reward is in addition to any XP they earned from creatures defeated during the storm.

RESZAVASS

CHAPTER 2

Beyond the Colony

With the first of many storms passed and Pridon's Hearth safe for the moment, the PCs have a chance to rest, sell treasure, shop, and heal. Though the faith of Abadar forbids providing free services, Banker Baldra Siferth considers the PCs' actions in the town over the past 24 hours more than enough payment to justify casting up to four *cure light wounds* spells, and up to four *cure moderate wounds* or *lesser restoration* spells on the PCs' behalf.

In the storm's wake, Count Lethar Narsus summons the town council to meet in his estate and discuss recent events. Sheriff Adaela invites the PCs to attend, both in recognition of their aid and so they can testify regarding the situation in Fort Breakthrough.

The Town Council

While the Narsus family rules Pridon's Hearth without official oversight, save what little Sargava imposes, Lethar Narsus leans heavily on a circle of advisors he calls his town council. The count assembles everyone of relative influence in town, hoping to pool their knowledge and decide how best to defend the settlement and surrounding farms. In addition to the count and the sheriff, Banker Baldra Sifreth attends, as does the count's financial advisor, Hamsa Gadd, thanks to her economic interest in the community and her ill-fated explorations of the surrounding region.

Count Narsus is a well-intentioned but inexperienced leader, and has spent the last several weeks holed up in his mansion, fearing the predations of the troll Graular.

INTRODUCTION

CHAPTER 1:
THE DELUGE

CHAPTER 2:
BEYOND THE COLONY

CHAPTER 3:
THE SKY TEMPEST TEMPLE

APPENDIX 1:
PRIDON'S HEARTH

APPENDIX 2:
BESTIARY

He ultimately wants Pridon's Hearth to grow into a place where hard work can secure any family (including his own) a legacy and land for generations, and eagerly announces a plan to explore the jungle himself. The other attendees—especially Hamsa Gadd—quickly convince him to leave such drastic actions to professionals. Everyone assembled agrees that the adventurers who reported the massacre at Fort Breakthrough and are now deputies of the sheriff are the most qualified to investigate this disaster.

Hearing of lizardfolk involvement at Fort Breakthrough and seeing Reszavass in Pridon's Hearth convince Sheriff Adaela that the Mireborn lizardfolk are somehow responsible for the storm. Adaela knows little of the Mireborn, having only heard rumors of the lizardfolk's presence in the northern jungle. Early scouting expeditions conducted years ago reported seasonal camps to the northwest, near some Ghol-Gan ruins, and to the northeast, near a bubbling tar pit, but never any farther south.

Hamsa agrees that the Mireborn are involved, but refuses to rule out the Song'o as coconspirators, tossing the PCs a red herring in hopes of delaying their investigation. She encourages the PCs to visit the nearby halfling village of Cahshil and demand answers. If the PCs inquire after her own expedition, Hamsa obscures the truth, reporting that the Song'o ambushed them and killed everyone. She claims the raid happened at night, before she could take her morning bearings, and that she's unsure where the expedition had camped for the night, except that it was east of town.

Finding the Mireborn lair in the lands surrounding Pridon's Hearth and stopping the sinister magic they use to control the weather is the utmost priority. Count Narsus offers a substantial reward for the defeat of the Mireborn, though he's skittish about the exact amount, stating he'd need to contact Baron Utilinus in Eleder to request additional gold for saving an outpost of Sargava. If pressed, the count offers 5,000 gp to anyone who puts an end to the storms.

Aspis Interests

Unknown to Count Narsus but a relatively open secret around the rest of Pridon's Hearth, Hamsa Gadd is a member of the Aspis Consortium. She knows of the Sky Tempest Temple, but emphatically feels the temple's lost secrets are far more valuable to the Consortium than are the limited assets of one tiny colony, and hopes to prevent others from discovering the ruin until the Consortium sends her a full team to search and loot it.

LETHAR NARSUS

Regional Quests

In addition to their main quest of locating the Mireborn lizardfolk and stopping their ritual, the PCs can discover numerous optional quests around Pridon's Hearth. These quests are offered by NPCs in town, many of whom the PCs have already met.

The Cobalt Eye: Several people report seeing the ship the *Cobalt Eye* run aground west of town during the storm, and Count Narsus asks the PCs to investigate, offer assistance to any survivors, and retrieve a copy of the ship's passenger list so he can notify the families of those who perished. *Reward*: 1,200 XP, plus 1,000 gp.

Expedition Investigation: Kanjo Arram was the apprentice of a cleric named Magdi Kukoyi, who vanished during a recent expedition, leaving Kanjo penniless in a strange land. He asks the PCs to find Magdi's expedition and return his master's coin pouch so he can afford to return home, and the cleric's holy symbol of Gozreh so he can present it to his master's next of kin. *Reward*: 1,200 XP.

Family Affairs: Sheriff Adaela's cousin, Jheri "One Arm" Praet, runs a dika plantation along the marsh northeast of town. She asks the PCs to check in on him and make sure that he's all right after the storm. *Reward*: 800 XP, plus 400 gp.

Muhdzuzi's Escort: If Muhdzuzi survived and isn't held captive in town, he requests to be escorted home to Cahshil, promising rewards of wisdom and courage if the PCs agree. *Reward*: 800 XP, plus a *headband of inspired wisdom +2* and four *potions of remove fear*.

Site of Interest: Mr. Blackwell approaches after hearing "around town" that they'll be visiting the Ghol-Gan ruins, and informs the PCs he'll pay handsomely for any intact archaeological artifacts they recover. *Reward*: 1,200 XP, plus 2,500 gp.

Hamsa remains indecisive about how to handle this strange situation. Sending gullible adventurers to clear out the Mireborn infestation that slaughtered her own expedition seems like the easiest way to reclaim the Sky Tempest Temple, but she's unwilling to risk outsiders reporting such a valuable find to Count Narsus and jeopardizing the Consortium's claim to the ruins. While she recognizes that the storms are almost certainly the result of rediscovered Storm Kindler rituals performed at the temple, Hamsa obscures its existence unless she can quietly recruit the PCs as loyal Aspis agents or else eliminate them.

Treasure: For the role they played in saving Pridon's Hearth, Count Narsus rewards each PC with 500 gp, as well as two *potions of barkskin* (CL 3rd), a *+1 chain shirt*, and 25 *+1 crossbow bolts* from his father's hunting supplies. He also offers the PCs the deed to a plot of land within the town walls, though the deed remains binding only if they erect a permanent structure on the land provided and either live or run a business there for 2 years.

If the PCs accept the greater quest to stop the storms surrounding Pridon's Hearth, Count Narsus awards them an immediate stipend of 500 gp each, intended to be used to purchase goods and services for their expedition, and a *bird feather token* in case of emergencies.

Exploring the Lower Korir River Delta

The territory around the town of Pridon's Hearth consists mostly of unexplored marshlands, tropical hummocks, and grassy lowlands, with the edge of the true jungle — known locally as the Jungle of Hungry Trees—beginning farther east. Rain blankets the area, varying only in intensity, with miserable spitting in the mornings, pounding downpours in the early afternoons, and mist rising off the marshes at random intervals. Many of the landscape's ancient trees have toppled or now lean at odd angles thanks to the thunderstorm that just roared

through the area. The PCs need to blaze their own trails for the most part, aside from the muddy road between Pridon's Hearth and the remnants of Fort Breakthrough.

Ire of the Storm uses a simplified version of the exploration rules detailed in *Pathfinder RPG Ultimate Campaign*, beginning on page 154. Each hex on the map requires 8 hours to cross thanks to the rugged terrain (or 5 hours on horseback), and 2 full days to completely explore (1 day on horseback). Because the PCs usually are given specific directions to landmarks or benefit from guides, they won't generally need to explore a hex to find major adventure objectives, aside from the Sky Tempest Temple (see area **M** on page 37).

Game Masters should roll for random encounters once per day or once per hex (if the PCs cross more than one hex in a day) as the PCs explore the region (see the sidebar on page 23). In addition to the standard random encounters, the two specific exploration encounters listed on page 23 can appear anywhere on the map, and four encounters in Pridon's Hearth occur as the PCs finish certain missions and return to town to heal or resupply (see area **H**). If PCs don't return to town, these encounters can easily come to them—Sheriff Adaela may travel out to Jheri's plantation to look after her cousin, or the Aspis agents may follow the PCs into the field to keep an eye on them.

The hex immediately surrounding Pridon's Hearth is already explored. PCs don't need to roll for random encounters when they traverse it, and do not earn gold or XP for exploring it.

Treasure: If PCs wish to explore the region in more depth, Count Narsus pays them a grant of 50 gp for every hex they explore and map in detail.

Story Award: For every hex the PCs explore (rather than just travel through), award them 25 XP in addition to any XP earned for any monsters or hazards they encounter.

MIREBORN RAIDERS (CR 4)

The remainder of Reszavass's raiding party continues to prowl the marsh and outlying farms, hoping to strike fear into the human settlers. They see a small group of traveling colonists as a perfect target.

Creatures: Ezevash—a lizardfolk barbarian—and two warriors continue to pillage the area even after their commander's death. The three aren't as cautious as they should be, given their dwindling numbers, and assume all humans are as soft as the farmers they keep dispatching.

EZEVASH	CR 2

XP 600
Lizardfolk vanguard (*Pathfinder RPG Monster Codex* 142)
hp 33

LIZARDFOLK (2)	CR 1

XP 400 each
hp 11 each (*Pathfinder RPG Bestiary* 195)

Treasure: The raiders carry their haul from looting several farms: a set of masterwork thieves' tools, a spyglass, and 212 gp.

SONG'O TRAPPERS (CR 3)

The Song'o of Cahshil (see area **I** on page 34) send out small groups through the nearby marshlands and jungle edges to hunt or trap prey and to gather food and other resources. Reclusive and wary, the halflings keep their distance from Pridon's Hearth and the plantations.

A group of Song'o trappers currently brave the rain and wind to search for food and survey the damage caused by the storm. These halflings wield a combination of spears and javelins, though their tactics rely mainly on swarming less aggressive and less powerful animals.

Creatures: Six Song'o halfling trappers traverse the region in a tight-knit group. They've had little success in finding food for the tribe; most smaller fauna having sought shelter farther inland. They're wary of tallfolk, and generally hide to observe strangers rather than confront them directly. Desperate for supplies, the trappers stalk the PCs until they make camp, then try to slip in unnoticed to steal food. The Song'o fight only if attacked, or if the PCs attempt to pursue them.

Korir Delta Encounters

As the PCs explore the area surrounding Pridon's Hearth, GMs should roll to see what dangers they find. At the GM's discretion, an encounter may indicate running into a creature they encountered in Chapter 1 but failed to defeat.

d%	Result
1–50	No encounter
51–60	Hazard
61–100	Monster

d%	Hazard	Avg. CR	Source
1–40	Shallow bog	1	*Core Rulebook* 427
41–70	Quicksand	2	*Core Rulebook* 427
71–85	Deadly gas	3	*Ultimate Campaign* 159
86–100	Camouflaged pit trap	3	*Core Rulebook* 420

d%	Monster	Avg. CR	Source
1–5	1 constrictor snake	2	*Bestiary* 255
6–10	2d4 dire rats	2	*Bestiary* 232
11–18	1d4 eaisge	2	See page 62
19–26	1 goliath frog	3	*Bestiary 5* 117
27–34	1 kawa akago	3	*Bestiary 5* 149
35–42	Song'o Trappers	3	See below
43–51	1 forest drake	4	*Bestiary 2* 107
52–60	1 gray ooze	4	*Bestiary* 166
61–69	1 leech swarm	4	*Bestiary* 187
70–78	Mireborn Raiders	4	See below
79–87	1d4 water leapers	4	*Bestiary 5* 275
88–92	1 giant frilled lizard	5	*Bestiary* 194
93–96	1d4 Med. air elementals	5	*Bestiary* 120
97–100	1d6 troodons	5	*Bestiary 5* 84

The halflings carry spring-loaded animal traps—acquired from foreign explorers—and deploy them around themselves if they suspect an attack. These steel-jawed traps are less powerful than bear traps, being designed for wolves, deer, and other game of a similar size, but function similarly.

SONG'O TRAPPERS (6)	CR 1/3

XP 135 each
Halfling warrior 1
CN Small humanoid (halfling)
Init +0; **Senses** Perception +2
DEFENSE
AC 14, touch 11, flat-footed 14 (+3 armor, +1 size)
hp 6 each (1d10+1)
Fort +4, **Ref** +1, **Will** +1; +2 vs. fear
OFFENSE
Speed 20 ft. (15 ft. in armor)
Melee spear +2 (1d6/×3)
Ranged net +2 (entangle)

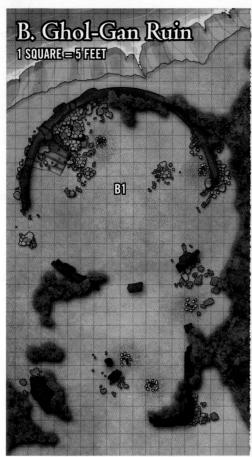

B. Ghol-Gan Ruin
1 SQUARE = 5 FEET

B1

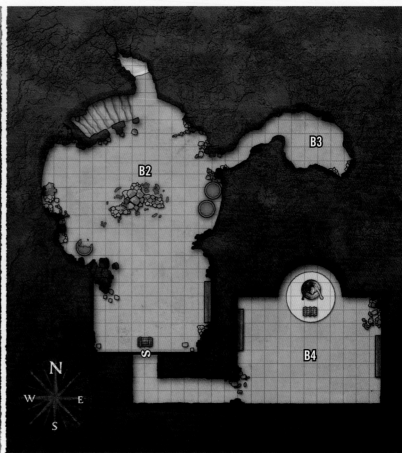

B3

B2

B4

TACTICS

During Combat The Song'o aren't fearsome, and rely on cleverness and tactics if confronted. They try to lure aggressive foes into traps, or engulf them in nets before closing to melee combat.

Morale A Song'o trapper flees if she is reduced to 2 hit points or fewer.

STATISTICS

Str 10, **Dex** 11, **Con** 13, **Int** 10, **Wis** 11, **Cha** 10

Base Atk +1; **CMB** +0; **CMD** 10

Feats Exotic Weapon Proficiency (net)

Skills Acrobatics +2 (–9 when jumping), Climb +6, Perception +2, Survival +1, Stealth +4 Swim +4; **Racial Modifiers** +2 Acrobatics, +2 Climb, +2 Perception

Languages Halfling, Polyglot

Gear mwk wooden armor^{UE}, net, spear, animal snares, flint and steel, spring-loaded trap, waterskin, Song'o necklace (worth 15 gp)

SPRING-LOADED TRAP	CR —

Type mechanical; **Perception** DC 15; **Disable Device** DC 15

EFFECTS

Trigger location; **Reset** manual

Effect Atk +10 melee (1d8+2); sharp jaws spring shut around the target's ankle and halve the target's base speed (or hold the target immobile if the trap is attached to a solid object);

the target can escape with a successful DC 15 Disable Device check, DC 20 Escape Artist check, or DC 20 Strength check.

Treasure: The trappers carry a *tree feather token* for emergency shelter, and offer it as a sign of friendship if the PCs make peaceful contact with them.

Development: The Song'o begin as unfriendly toward the PCs, but the PCs can shift their attitude to indifferent and at least convince them to communicate with a successful DC 20 Diplomacy check. If the PCs offer at least 12 days' worth of food, they gain a +6 circumstance bonus on skill checks to influence the Song'o. If the PCs make the Song'o friendly, the Song'o offer to escort the newcomers back with them to Cahshil (area **I**), or to escort Muhdzuzi back if he still travels with the PCs.

Story Award: Should the PCs negotiate peacefully with the Song'o, award them XP as if they defeated the hunting party in combat.

B. GHOL-GAN RUIN

The cyclops race once maintained a vast empire, ranging from the borders of the modern Sodden Lands and all along the western fringes of the Mwangi Expanse. Many ruins of lost Ghol-Gan still exist, and boast impressive treasures. Ghol-Gan didn't expand far south of what is now Sargava, though the cyclopes did perform their

INTRODUCTION

CHAPTER 1:
THE DELUGE

CHAPTER 2:
BEYOND THE COLONY

CHAPTER 3:
THE SKY TEMPEST TEMPLE

APPENDIX 1:
PRIDON'S HEARTH

APPENDIX 2:
BESTIARY

own exploration and trade up and down the west coast of Garund, leaving a variety of small outposts and settlements in their wake.

The ruin that stands along the coast here is the remains of an ancient lighthouse the cyclops used to navigate the coast. Most of the building collapsed millennia ago, but the magical stone of its foundations kept the cliff from eroding and protected the basement and a few stubborn walls. Beyond that, however, all that remains of this Ghol-Gan outpost is tumbled stones and a small cellar.

B1. Upper Ruins (CR 3)

Great blocks of stone, long crumbled and overgrown, wall in what is now merely a clearing. Vague hints of color still stain the walls here and there—the clearest paintings depict one-eyed people sailing and reading the stars. More recent paintings below depict lizardfolk hunting sharks and roasting large, white slabs of flesh.

These overgrown ruins were used as a seasonal camp by the Mireborn tribe for generations to take advantage of the mating run of bull sharks every year. If the PCs explore the area, they find fishing nets and spears, as well as wooden racks used to dry the season's catch. However, a successful DC 15 Survival check reveals signs of use within the last 6 weeks, long after the season for the bull shark runs depicted in the lizardfolk paintings—the Mireborn retreated here after their final loss to the Blackbruise Brood.

A few scattered bones can be identified as those of lizardfolk with a successful DC 16 Knowledge (local) or Heal check.

Creature: A single assassin vine, which moved into the area to feed off the scraps the Mireborn left behind, hides amid the foliage-covered stones. The plant slithers throughout the ruins, growing hungry now that its easy access to food is gone. The storm activity keeps other animals away from the coast, so the assassin vine is peckish, and attacks any living creature it finds.

ASSASSIN VINE	CR 3

XP 800
hp 30 (*Pathfinder RPG Bestiary* 22)

Development: Several recent paintings here give clues to the location of the Sky Tempest Temple, showing a small river and several other local features, but give no wider context. To use this information to locate the temple, the PCs need to learn its general location from either the exile Achahut (see area **E3**) or from Hamsa Gadd's notes (see the Development section of The Serpent Strikes on page 34).

A stairway leading down is plainly visible beneath some rubble along the northern wall. The wall above collapsed only a decade ago, and after the Mireborn lost

two warriors trying to clear it, they resolved to leave the passage sealed. Clearing the rubble away requires a total of three successful DC 17 Strength checks.

Story Award: If the PCs learn the details of the location of the Sky Tempest Temple, award them an extra 1,600 XP.

B2. Lighthouse Basement (CR 5)

Black stone lines the walls of this rubble-strewn chamber. Bundles of fishing supplies—faded and dusty—rest near the base of the stairs, while the broken remains of far older pottery line the walls. Two clay urns, each the size of a person, still stand to the east near a natural opening in the stone wall, and a dusty chest lies near the southern wall. To the north, some sort of animal-dug burrow descends into brackish water.

Once the storeroom for the now-destroyed lighthouse, this chamber is carved from the rock of the cliff face and lined with basalt. It extends southward, eventually opening up to a smaller room beyond. The shattered urns were used to store food, wine, and lamp oil. The two remaining urns cracked centuries ago, spilling their rancid wine across the floor.

The opening to the north is an entrance dug by the basement's inhabitant. The burrow leads through 30 feet of underwater tunnel before emerging into the sea. The underwater entrance is impossible to spot from land. A secret door is concealed in the southern wall; noticing it requires a successful DC 18 Perception check.

Creatures: A mimic moved into this ruin shortly after the main entrance collapsed, squeezing through the rubble and eventually digging a permanent aquatic tunnel so it could come and go freely. It has currently retreated to security of the sealed basement after eating two lizardfolk. The mimic disguises itself as a treasure chest if it hears strangers nearby, and attacks if anyone approaches it.

MIMIC	CR 4

XP 1,200
hp 52 (*Pathfinder RPG Bestiary* 205)

B3. The Den

This winding chamber is roughly carved from the limestone, and widens into a large chamber lined with dead vegetation and animal bones. A faded white paste coats the walls.

The mimic in area **B2** carved this nest to store food and produce young years ago. With a successful DC 19 Knowledge (dungeoneering) check, a PC identifies the white paste on the walls as the spawning protoplasm that mimics use to bud their young. A successful DC 15 Perception check reveals unusual, needlelike teeth amid the animal bones—all that remain of the mimic plasmoids too slow to escape their ravenous mother.

Development: If the PCs enter this chamber without encountering the mimic in area **B2**, the aberration moves in closer. When the PCs emerge, the treasure chest in area **B2** has vanished, but with a successful DC 15 Perception check, a PC notices that there are now three intact urns rather than two; recalling which of these urns were present earlier (and which is the impostor) requires a successful DC 14 Intelligence or Wisdom check.

B4. Shrine to the Sun and Moon (CR 5)

Stone tablets the size of tabletops line the basalt walls here, each engraved with meticulous script and illuminated by the flickering light of two small, glowing points orbiting the statue of an imposing, single-eyed giant. A vast skeletal figure kneels position in the center of the chamber.

JHERI PRAET

This chamber housed the lighthouse's chapel to the Sun and the Moon, as well as any valuables its Ghol-Gan overseers thought to conceal from pirates. The last cyclops lighthouse keeper came down here to ensure the records of the lighthouse were preserved.

The tablets along the walls of this chamber are the preserved knowledge of the Ghol-Gan sentinels who oversaw the lighthouse's operation. Written in Cyclops, the tablets record the coming and going of Ghol-Gan vessels in the region and various holy days and celestial events observed from the once-grand tower. A few also detail the locations of Ghol-Gan expeditions and remote trading posts that could prove valuable to anyone hunting lost treasures.

Creature: The last keeper left behind to staff the lighthouse died ages ago after sealing himself and the empire's records in the shrine. Though he was kindly in life, a modicum of energy and resentment at his abandonment now animates his skeletal remains to test any intruders.

THE LAST KEEPER	CR 5

XP 1,600
Unique cyclops skeleton (*Pathfinder RPG Bestiary* 52, 250)
NE Large undead
Init +4; **Senses** darkvision 60 ft.; Perception +8

DEFENSE

AC 17, touch 9, flat-footed 17 (+6 armor, +2 natural, –1 size)
hp 56 (10d8+11)
Fort +3, **Ref** +3, **Will** +7
DR 5/bludgeoning; **Immune** cold, undead traits

OFFENSE

Speed 30 ft. (20 ft. in armor)
Melee 2 claws +11 (1d6+5)
Space 10 ft.; **Reach** 10 ft.

STATISTICS

Str 21, **Dex** 10, **Con** —, **Int** —, **Wis** 10, **Cha** 12
Base Atk +7; **CMB** +13; **CMD** 23
Feats Improved Initiative
Skills Acrobatics –4 (–8 to jump), Perception +8;
Racial Modifiers +8 Perception
Languages Common, Cyclops, Giant
Gear breastplate

Treasure: Scattered around the cyclopean statue are 10 +1 *monstrous humanoid-bane* arrows, 50 saucer-sized golden coins (worth 10 gp each), and a Large +1 *kukri* inscribed with lunar imagery. The pale blue and pale yellow motes orbiting the statue's head are both *ioun torches* (*Ultimate Equipment* 305).

Development: The tablets here can be returned to Mr. Blackwell in Pridon's Hearth to complete the Site of Interest quest (see page 21).

C. JHERI'S PLANTATION (CR 5)

"Plantation" is a generous descriptor the locals apply to this log cabin and the surrounding stands of dika trees. The owner, Jheri "One Arm" Praet, is a local legend to the people of Pridon's Hearth, thanks to the endless speculation over how he lost his arm—a story both Jheri and his cousin the sheriff refuse to discuss. Jheri has lived well since arriving in Pridon's Hearth, and having found an ideal location to grow crops (dika fruit and seeds), he supplied the settlers with cheap and tasty calories during the colony's difficult first few years.

The recent storm damaged Jheri's cabin, tearing away part of the thatched palm-leaf roof and several shutters. Everything is quiet when the PCs arrive. The door is closed but unlocked. A single room makes up most of the interior, save for a large storage closet in the far corner. The rest of the furniture inside the cabin is upended. Jheri is hiding within the closet, and if he hears anyone rummaging through the cabin, he calls out feebly for assistance.

Creature: At the height of the storm's landfall, the winds caught a vicious marsh-dwelling ooze and splattered it against Jheri's cabin, allowing the creature to seep in through the damaged roof. It later descended upon Jheri, and caught by surprise, he hurriedly barricaded himself inside the closet, where he has remained ever since. The ooze patiently waits just outside the closet, looking like a muddy puddle to casual observers, as Jheri slowly succumbs to dehydration and disease within.

OCHRE JELLY	CR 5

XP 1,600
hp 30 (*Pathfinder RPG Bestiary* 218)

INTRODUCTION

CHAPTER 1:
THE DELUGE

CHAPTER 2:
BEYOND THE COLONY

CHAPTER 3:
THE SKY TEMPEST TEMPLE

APPENDIX 1:
PRIDON'S HEARTH

APPENDIX 2:
BESTIARY

Treasure: Jheri keeps a wooden chest hidden under his bed (Perception DC 20), containing his amassed wealth and family keepsakes. The chest contains 106 gp, 502 sp, and a number of carved ivory game tokens and a playing board (worth 150 gp as a set). It also holds Jheri's father's spellbook, which includes the following spells: 1st—*alarm, comprehend languages, identify, magic weapon, unseen servant;* 2nd—*minor image, protection from arrows, see invisibility, spectral hand;* 3rd—*dispel magic, heroism, slow.* The spellbook is locked with an average quality lock (Disable Device DC 25) and is worth 500 gp. Jheri knew little of his father's magical talents, keeping this spellbook only as a memento.

Development: If the PCs defeat the ooze or lure it away, they can find Jheri lying in the closet, shivering from what had been a mild case of red ache he contracted on his muddy farm. Without food, water, or proper rest, he was unable to resist the disease, which ravaged his body. Thanks to the dehydration and disease, his Strength score is reduced to 2, and he has only 1 hit point remaining. The PCs can assist Jheri with a successful DC 15 Heal check, or by administering a dose of antiplague[UE], giving him enough strength to safely travel to Pridon's Hearth and recuperate with his cousin. Investigating Jheri's fate completes the Family Affairs quest (see page 21).

If the PCs loot Jheri's trunk while he lives, he reports the theft to the sheriff and she withholds the cash reward for looking into her cousin's fate. If the PCs assist Jheri in reaching town and don't loot his trunk, he offers them 100 gp and his father's spellbook as a reward for saving him, in addition to the reward Adaela promised.

D. THE FIRST COLONY

The roofs of this circle of timber-and-mortar homes have all collapsed, and once-vibrant paint peels away in long strips. Rampant jungle growth obscures the remains of a well, benches, and a human-shaped statue.

When the original generation of Storm Kindlers arrived in the Korir River Delta, they established a village in which to live, farm, and study for the several years it took to erect the more remote temple. With the cult's destruction, the village quickly fell into ruin and was consumed by the wilderness, and today, 90 years later, all that remains are a few stone walls, rotted books, and broken crockery.

Treasure: A PC who succeeds at a DC 17 Perception check uncovers a sagging secret compartment in the largest house, which contains several papers too decayed to read, a *+1 kukri*, and a silver holy symbol shaped like a notched shark's fin (worth 25 gp). With a successful DC 15 Knowledge (religion) check, a PC identifies it as a holy symbol of Kelizandri, the evil Elemental Lord of Water.

Development: Clearing the statue of the vines covering it reveals a hardwood carving, masculine on one side and feminine on the other. With a successful DC 10 Knowledge (religion) check, a PC identifies the figure as Gozreh, the god of weather and the sea. An inscription in Kelish at the statue's base reads, "The Wind and the Wave gave us the Eye that we might see, and we journey here so that two Eyes may gaze upon creation. Founded 4621 AR."

Searching most of the ruins reveals little of value, though a PC who succeeds at a DC 12 Perception check discovers an old journal wrapped in oilcloth. Though it's badly damaged, at least a few entries remain legible, mostly discussing the severe weather in Lirgen and daily routines. The final legible entry reads, "...have decided to exile Chitauli rather than acknowledge his insight and take the bold steps needed to survive. The Eye is a sign from the Wind and the Waves, and if we wish to truly take control of our destiny, we must master the same energies that birthed it. These conservative old fools are content to wring their hands and wait while Lirgen rots around us, and so the true Storm Kindlers depart for the south. Chitauli has agreed to guide..."

Story Award: If the PCs uncover the statue of Gozreh or find the Storm Kindler journal, award them 800 XP.

E. TAR PITS

Mounds of enormous bones litter the ground surrounding this bubbling tar seep. The dinosaurs of the delta have long used this area as a graveyard, journeying to the area as they grow old or sick. Many scavengers dwell near or visit the macabre piles, including the Mireborn lizardfolk, who visit the tar pits annually to inter their dead in the black lake and forage bones, teeth, and claws.

Patches of black tar fill the area. The tar pools count as difficult terrain, and any creatures that enters a tar-filled square must succeed at a DC 14 Reflex save or become entangled. An entangled creature can escape the tar with a successful Strength or Escape Artist check. The DC for a Small or Medium creature to escape is 13; the DC increases by 2 for every size category larger than Medium an entangled creature is.

E1. Mireborn Exile Camp (CR 5)

Battered by relentless winds and drizzle, a campfire burns sullenly under the cover of immense rib bones the size of small trees. A handful of javelins are piled beside the fire.

Not all the Mireborn accepted Daruthek's plan to wipe the humans from the region. After hours of argument broke down into violence, Chief Shathva exiled the dissidents and their de facto leader, the dour Achahut. Bereft of tribe and purpose, the exiles set up camp in their ancestral graveyard, and now grimly wait to join the bones of their ancestors. The lizardfolk here consider themselves already dead for earning their clan's hatred, and wish to be left in solitude.

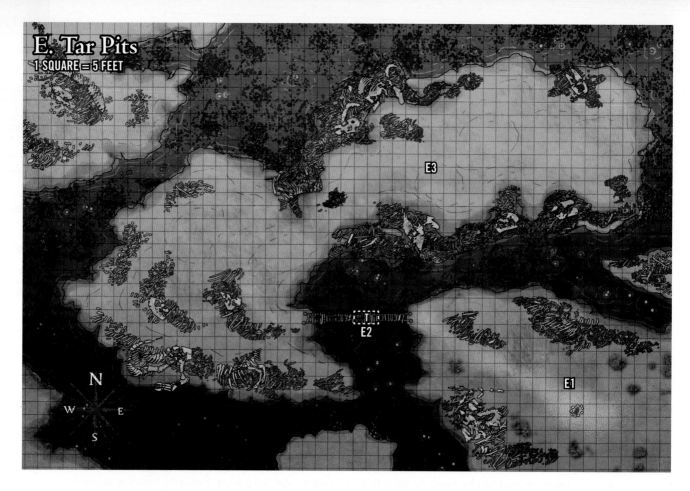

E. Tar Pits
1 SQUARE = 5 FEET

E3

E2

E1

N
W   E
S

Creatures: Three lizardfolk exiles maintain a small camp here, along with their well-trained hunting lizard. The Mireborn attempt to keep their rapidly dwindling fire alight in the battering winds and drizzle, using the bubbling tar as a smoky but stable fuel. While they don't support utilizing dark magic to exterminate their enemies, they have no love for invaders, and are initially hostile toward any humanoids they encounter. Unless given extraordinary reasons not to, the hunters attack any non-lizardfolk newcomers on sight, fighting until one of their number falls. Once outsiders prove dangerous, they flee over a bone bridge (see area **E2**) to find Achahut in area **E3**.

LIZARDFOLK (3)	CR 1

XP 400 each

hp 11 each (*Pathfinder RPG Bestiary* 195)
Ranged longbow +1 (1d8/×3)
Gear longbow with 10 arrows (replaces javelins)

MONITOR LIZARD	CR 2

XP 600

hp 22 (*Pathfinder RPG Bestiary* 194)

Treasure: A woven sack contains the items the lizardfolk brought with them: four *potions of cure light wounds*, a *potion of neutralize poison*, and a jar of *defoliant polish*^{UE}.

Development: If captured or compelled to talk, the former Mireborn explain the desperation of their tribe after their humiliating and costly defeat by the Blackbruise Brood boggards, how Chieftain Shathva traveled south to find shelter while her people healed and recovered their numbers, and Swamp-Speaker Daruthek's proposal to drive out the human settlers, who would invariably threaten their safety. A PC who succeeds at a DC 18 Diplomacy or Intimidate check also detects the lizardfolk's belief that a rift is forming between Shathva and Daruthek, who is conjuring the storms engulfing the region. Beyond this, these exiles know little else.

E2. Bone Bridge (CR 3)

Oversized femurs and ribs have been bound together into a ladderlike structure supported by log rafts that float atop the tar, creating a ramshackle bridge to the adjoining island.

Traps: The Mireborn visit Ossuary Island often to scavenge dinosaur remains, and constructed this bridge generations ago to avoid the need to wade through the scalding tar. They also trapped the bridge to discourage poachers. Creatures in the area of the trap risk being hit by darts fired from a concealed mechanism in the bone pile to the north.

HAIL OF DARTS TRAP	CR 3

Type mechanical; **Perception** DC 20; **Disable Device** DC 20

EFFECTS

Trigger location; **Reset** manual

Effect hail of darts (Atk +10 ranged, 1d4+1 darts per target for 1d3 damage each plus small centipede poison); multiple targets (all targets in a 5-ft.-by-15-ft. area)

E3. Ossuary Island (CR 6)

Some strange radiance of this island attracts dinosaurs as they near death, spurring them to brave wading through the tar shallows to the northwest and wait for the inevitable alongside the bones of their ancestors.

Creatures: While most of the exiles simply wait for the end, their leader Achahut seeks out her death by challenging greater and greater beasts to battle. By the time the PCs arrive, the warrior is engaged in combat with a half-mad ankylosaurus that journeyed to the tar pits to die following its infection by Mwangi brain worms.

Achahut attacks anyone who might interfere with her fight, and the dinosaur lashes out wildly at any creatures it sees. The PCs can wait to see who wins, or engage, turning the battle into a three-way fight to the death.

ACHAHUT	CR 4

XP 1,200

Female lizardfolk fighter 3 (*Pathfinder RPG Bestiary* 195)

CN Medium humanoid (reptilian)

Init +3; **Senses** Perception +1

DEFENSE

AC 19, touch 9, flat-footed 19 (+5 armor, −1 Dex, +5 natural)

hp 43 (5 HD; 2d8+3d10+18)

Fort +9, **Ref** +0, **Will** +4 (+1 vs. fear)

OFFENSE

Speed 30 ft., swim 15 ft.

Melee mwk heavy pick +9 (1d6+3/×4), bite +5 (1d4+1), claws +5 (1d4+1)

Ranged javelin +3 (1d6+3)

TACTICS

During Combat Achahut relies on her Power Attack feat to deal as much damage as she can.

Morale Achahut wants only to fight to the death.

STATISTICS

Str 17, **Dex** 8, **Con** 16, **Int** 8, **Wis** 12, **Cha** 13

Base Atk +4; **CMB** +7; **CMD** 16

Feats Improved Initiative, Iron Will, Multiattack, Power Attack, Weapon Focus (heavy pick)

Skills Acrobatics +2, Handle Animal +5, Intimidate +7, Survival +5, Swim +10; **Racial Modifiers** +4 Acrobatics

Languages Draconic

SQ armor training 1, hold breath

Combat Gear elixir of hiding, elixir of swimming, elixir of vision; **Other Gear** +1 hide armor, javelin (5), mwk heavy pick, deinonychus claws (7; worth 10 gp each), tyrannosaur fang dagger (worth 100 gp)

SICK ANKYLOSAURUS	CR 5

XP 1,600

Ankylosaurus (*Pathfinder RPG Bestiary* 83)

hp 75 (currently 60)

SPECIAL ABILITIES

Brain Worms (Ex) These ravaging parasites impose the sickened condition, and decrease the Fortitude DC of the beast's stun special ability to 18. This reduces the beast's CR by 1.

Treasure: The tar pit is a treasure trove of strange trophies, though much of it is stained by tar fumes from the bubbling lake of asphalt that surrounds it, and the choicest remnants are normally claimed by the Mireborn each year. If PCs want to scavenge, a successful DC 19 Craft (armor or weapons), Knowledge (nature), or Survival check reveals enough material to build one weapon or suit of armor from bone (*Pathfinder RPG Ultimate Equipment* 52). The dinosaur bones take enchantments readily, and can be crafted into +1 armor for 10% less than the usual cost. This does not reduce the cost of subsequent improvements. Each check to scavenge takes 2 hours.

Development: Should the PCs attack the ankylosaurus, Achahut bellows, "The great beast is *my* death! Do not make me regret speaking on behalf of your wretched people!" If she survives the fight, the hulking lizardfolk turns to the newcomers and announces, "I have no people and no worth. The least your kind can do to repay my sacrifice is deliver me an honorable death in battle." If the PCs ask, she makes no attempt to disguise her contempt for humans and their "variations" (i.e., other nonreptilian humanoids). Regardless, Achahut details how the exiles came to dwell in the tar pits after opposing "the feather-backed coward Daruthek," a mutant lizardfolk guiding their tribe to war so the Mireborn can claim the area as their new home.

Achahut stood against Daruthek's plan, believing her people to be excellent hunters but finding no honor or purpose in conquest—a purely human vice, in her opinion. The old soldier is even willing to provide directions to the hidden Sky Tempest Temple (area **M**)—if the humans agree to show mercy to her tribe and target only Daruthek and his corrupted followers. However, she can offer only a general location, and lacks enough detailed knowledge to guide the PCs directly to it. To find the temple's exact location, the PCs need to find the maps at the old lizardfolk camp in the Ghol-Gan ruin (see area **B**).

Achahut demands an honorable death by battle from the PCs in exchange for the information she provides, and won't hold back in the fight. Without a tribe, she is without purpose in life. She can be persuaded to join a new "tribe," such as the PCs or Pridon's Hearth, with a successful DC 19 Diplomacy check, though she finds the idea distasteful and confusing.

INTRODUCTION

CHAPTER 1: THE DELUGE

CHAPTER 2: BEYOND THE COLONY

CHAPTER 3: THE SKY TEMPEST TEMPLE

APPENDIX 1: PRIDON'S HEARTH

APPENDIX 2: BESTIARY

Story Award: If the PCs deal with Achahut peacefully, award them 1,200 XP as if they defeated her in combat. If the PCs learn the general location of the Sky Tempest Temple—either here or from Hamsa Gadd (see area **H**)—award them an extra 1,600 XP.

F. CORACAP ROCK (CR 4)

The landscape along this bend in the northern river fork breaks up into dozens of small islands crowded with trees. Countless tropical birds roost in these islands, but one island—called Coracap Rock by many local tribes—hosts a large flock of mischievous coral capuchins.

Creatures: Coral capuchins—a local breed of magical beasts that resemble playful, flying monkey-fish—roost here to lay eggs and rear their young. While the storms have driven most of the beasts deeper into the jungle for safety, a trio of stubborn young parents has remained behind to guard the clutch of eggs.

Naturally thieving little creatures, the coral capuchins attempt to swipe shiny things from any explorers they encounter, and waste no time to stealing whatever they can should they catch sight of the PCs.

CORAL CAPUCHIN

CORAL CAPUCHINS (3)	CR 1

XP 400 each

Pathfinder Adventure Path #58: Island of Empty Eyes 80

N Tiny magical beast (aquatic)

Init +3; **Senses** darkvision 60 ft., low-light vision; Perception +1

DEFENSE

AC 15, touch 15, flat-footed 12 (+3 Dex, +2 size)

hp 13 each (2d10+2)

Fort +4, **Ref** +6, **Will** +1

Weaknesses moisture dependency

OFFENSE

Speed 30 ft., climb 30 ft., fly 40 ft. (good), swim 30 ft.

Melee bite +7 (1d3–2 plus cursed bite)

Space 2-1/2 ft.; **Reach** 0 ft.

Special Attacks cursed bite

STATISTICS

Str 6, **Dex** 17, **Con** 12, **Int** 6, **Wis** 13, **Cha** 7

Base Atk +2; **CMB** +3; **CMD** 11

Feats Weapon Finesse

Skills Climb +6, Fly +11, Sleight of Hand +8, Stealth +15

(+19 within coral reefs), Swim +6; **Racial Modifiers** +4 Sleight of Hand, +4 Stealth within coral reefs

SQ amphibious

SPECIAL ABILITIES

Cursed Bite (Su) A coral capuchin can deliver a bite that bestows some of the creature's benefits and weaknesses upon the victim. The curse delivered by this bite persists for 1d6 hours, and cannot affect the same creature more than once in a 24-hour period. Affected creatures begin drying out when exposed to air, but can hold their breath for double the normal amount of time. Targets of this cursed bite take 1d6 points of damage for every 10 minutes they are out of water, though spending a full-round action to bathe the victim in any sort of water halts this damage. Victims must succeed at a DC 12 Constitution check to avoid this effect. *Remove curse* ends this curse's effect as normal. The save DC is Constitution-based.

Moisture Dependency (Ex) A coral capuchin can breathe both air and water and survive indefinitely on land, but the creature must regularly be either submerged in water or thoroughly wetted down, or else it dries out in the air. A coral capuchin can survive out of water for a number of hours of equal to its Constitution score before it takes any negative effects. After this time, the creature takes 1d6 points of damage for every hour it remains dry. Bathing the creature in water of any sort resets this time frame.

Treasure: Coral capuchins are compulsive pickpockets, thieving items from wanderers in the jungle to decorate their nests and attract mates. Searching all the nests takes an hour, but turns up 49 gp, 174 sp, 770 cp, 12 masterwork arrows, a masterwork light pick, a *potion of enlarge person*, a silver locket containing a tuft of red hair (worth 25 gp), and eight freshwater pearls (worth 5 gp each).

Development: Most of the flock abandoned their eggs in the face of the worsening weather, and the severe winds and driving rain have since knocked many of those eggs to the ground. A total of 29 eggs remain. The PCs can trade these eggs to the tojanida Guughwa (see area **J**) or sell them (for 5 gp each) in Pridon's Hearth, where the Stone Hall puts them to similar use. Alternatively, a spellcaster with the Improved Familiar feat can hatch one if her alignment is within one step of neutral, gaining a mercurial coral capuchin as her familiar. Coral capuchins cannot be reared as animal companions.

G. THE COBALT EYE (CR 4)

The *Cobalt Eye* was a sailing ship that set out from the Shackles to bring a cartography team from Andoran to the Laughing Jungle. Caught in the recent storm, the ship ran aground, then broke up under the battering of the storm surge. In the end, the crew and passengers died gruesome deaths—be it at the hands of the elements or each other.

Creatures: Most of the *Cobalt Eye's* passengers were slain by the ravaging storm as it made landfall, and their bodies have been scattered throughout the region. These slain travelers arose as undead creatures known as eaisges—bloated bodies animated by foul waters from the Elemental Plane of Water. The PCs may recognize one of the unfortunate dead: the huntress Umuzu, a Zenj woman who boarded the *Cobalt Eye* shortly after the PCs landed in Pridon's Hearth.

Two eaisges and four zombies prowl the wreck of the *Cobalt Eye*. All of these animated corpses shuffle to attack the first living creature they spot, fighting until destroyed.

EAISGES (2)	CR 1

XP 400 each

hp 16 each (see page 62)

HUMAN ZOMBIES (2)	CR 1/2

XP 200 each

hp 12 each (*Pathfinder RPG Bestiary* 288)

Treasure: Searching the wrecked hull takes roughly an hour. Amid the wreckage, the PCs find Umuzu's hunting bow (a *+1 composite longbow* [*+2 Str*]), four *potions of cure light wounds*, 1,632 gp, 22,350 sp, 21 pp, six quartz gems (worth 20 gp each), and a monkey-shaped bone idol (worth 75 gp).

The PCs also discover a large stash of building materials in the cargo hold, which may prove useful to Pridon's Hearth. If the PCs return the 2,000 pounds of lumber, pitch, nails, canvas, ropes, and tools to town or they direct the townsfolk to the location of the supplies, a grateful Count Narsus rewards them with 1,000 gp.

Development: A PC who succeeds at a DC 12 Perception check discovers the ship's waterlogged but still legible passenger list within the broken captain's cabin. Returning this list to Count Narsus completes the quest The Cobalt Eye (see page 21).

H. PRIDON'S HEARTH

Pridon's Hearth remains relatively stable as the PCs explore the region, but politics still grind away, especially as the Aspis Consortium grows nervous and begins making efforts to recruit or eliminate the PCs. Independent adventurers exploring the region may jeopardize the Consortium's claim to the Sky Tempest Temple, and revelations that the Consortium knew the Mireborn were growing increasingly violent could easily sour their influence with Count Narsus.

The GM should stage the following encounters as appropriate whenever the PCs return to Pridon's Hearth. They are listed roughly in chronological order, rather than by their locations within the town.

The Sheriff's Invitation

Whether or not the PCs save Jheri Praet (see area **C**), Sheriff Adaela offers to thank them for attempting her quest with a private dinner in her humble home. If they agree, they find Adaela's cooking is exceptional even if the surroundings are cramped and still under construction, and she opens a bottle of quality Eleder whiskey to accompany the meal.

Over the course of the dinner, the PCs learn Adaela's history as a former holy warrior of Iomedae. She joined the order young, leaving home to train in Eleder. Afterward, she served her country as a soldier for years until her holy vows brought her to face to face with her sister, who had become a smuggler and major figure in a Crown's End Besmara cult. Unable to redeem her, Adaela finally forsook her vows, turned against her fellow soldiers, and let her sister flee to the Shackles. Given the circumstances, her sentence was lenient: enslavement to the Narsus family to compensate them for the goods stolen by the younger Praet sister. When Servius Narsus freed his slaves after bringing them to Pridon's Hearth, Adaela used her training to help keep the peace, and the count eventually appointed her sheriff despite her previous lapse in judgment.

Adaela discovered her sister died in a barroom brawl mere months after her escape. She now hopes to spend the remainder of her life building something new in Pridon's Hearth—ideally both a community and a family—and fears the growing storms could see the end of this last spark of hope in her life.

If the PCs have not yet noticed the Aspis Consortium's presence in town, Sheriff Adaela uses this opportunity to discuss her feelings on the organization. She believes the Consortium plans to make the count their puppet, or replace him if the colony's situation grows dire. She believes there is more to Hamsa Gadd's failed expedition than the woman reveals, and suspects that if any members of the Consortium's previous expedition still live, they could provide further insight into the organization's goals in the region. If the PCs still haven't spoken with Kanjo Arram (see the Expedition Investigation quest on page 21), she directs them to the youth.

Treasure: Adaela gives each PC a bottle of potent Sargavan ale (worth 50 gp). Drinking an entire bottle of ale provides a +1 morale bonus on all saving throws for 1 hour. If the PCs saved Jheri Praet's life, Sheriff Adaela also gifts them her old shield, a *+1 heavy steel shield* emblazoned with the Sargavan flag, in addition to the money she promised.

Story Award: If the PCs join the sheriff for dinner, award them an extra 800 XP.

INTRODUCTION

CHAPTER 1:
THE DELUGE

CHAPTER 2:
BEYOND THE COLONY

CHAPTER 3:
THE SKY TEMPEST TEMPLE

APPENDIX 1:
PRIDON'S HEARTH

APPENDIX 2:
BESTIARY

Additional Town Encounters

The PCs should feel comfortable returning to Pridon's Hearth at any point during their exploration to resupply, sell treasure, or heal. Reszavass's death inadvertently grants the village some protection from the tempest raging around it, magically holding the worst storms at bay for now. Several minor encounters are listed below, and can occur whenever the PCs return to town.

An Apology: Theos Votto (page 6) approaches the PCs during one of their visits—assuming the PCs spared the drunkard's life. He has since sobered up, and now lends his carpentry skills to the construction of new defenses. Theos apologizes for his previous actions, explaining his alcohol dependence as being related to the loss of his son and wife shortly after their arrival in town, and offers the PCs two *potions of touch of the sea*^{APG}, since they helped him stop "drowning his sorrows."

Homemade: Mirya Oyin (page 17) offers the adventurers a still-warm pie the next time they stop by her emporium, insisting Cassia "must have left it lying around in the mess" and that she "only just found it." If the PCs agree to take it off her hands, she offers them a 50 gp credit at the store.

Pretty Kitty: If the PCs saved Delour the cat during the storm, at some point they find the fat tabby tugging at their pants legs, begging for food. The cat follows them around town for an hour, until a haggard Maso Pareto catches up with them. Pareto thanks them again for finding his cat, and says he'll name the next litter of kittens after the town heroes.

Aspis Intrigue

Anytime after the town meeting, Hamsa Gadd invites the PCs to the count's estate for drinks to "thank them for their bold service to local business." She spends much of the dinner plying them with excellent Chelish wines and candied fruit, and focuses the conversation on the adventurers' pasts and their impressions of Pridon's Hearth thus far. If the PCs seem mercenary and not especially attached to the town or its people, she offers them a chance to work for her unnamed "benefactor," but if they seem attached to the community or burdened with morals, she instead resigns herself to have them observed—and likely eliminated—after she uses them to weaken the Mireborn tribe.

Hamsa speaks of her own past in vague terms, talking only about her "trouble in school" and her love of "field work." She refuses to discuss her failed expedition, saying it's "too painful to revisit." If the PCs have met Kanjo Arram and ask about Magdi Kukoyi, Hamsa acknowledges he was "brave until the end," and promises to furnish the boy with whatever funds he needs to return home, and a holy symbol he can claim belonged to his master. In reality, Hamsa simply orders her men to kill the apprentice and dump his body in the river after dark to prevent him from raising more questions (which the PCs may interrupt; see Aspis Assault below).

Story Award: If the PCs take the time to meet with Hamsa, award them 800 XP.

Aspis Assault (CR 4)

This event occurs after Hamsa Gadd discovers that Magdi Kukoyi's now-abandoned apprentice, Kanjo Arram, is still in town and asking questions—possibly when the PCs accidentally tell her as much while asking their own questions. Hamsa dispatches her few remaining Aspis agents to kill the young man and dump his body in the river. The PCs stumble across the attack in progress after dark one night while in town and have the chance to intercede, perhaps discovering in the process that Hamsa Gadd is less charitable than she claimed.

Alternatively, if the PCs are especially mercenary, Hamsa may dispatch them personally to kill Kanjo and prove their loyalty. In this case, the boy is easy enough to find— he stays at the Stone Hall and pays his keep by running errands day and night. Rather than fighting fellow Aspis agents, the PCs must eliminate three guards who interrupt their attack (use the same statistics as for the Aspis thugs).

Creatures: Three Aspis Consortium thugs posing as members of the town guard grabbed the young Kanjo as he was walking through the streets and shoved him into a darkened passage between two buildings. One thug stands as a lookout, while the other two try to keep Kanjo quiet and restrained long enough to slit his throat. As the PCs pass by, the cleric's apprentice lets out a cry for help that is quickly muffled.

ASPIS THUGS (3)	CR 1

XP 400 each
Human rogue 2
NE Medium humanoid (human)
Init +6; **Senses** Perception +5

DEFENSE
AC 16, touch 12, flat-footed 14 (+4 armor, +2 Dex)
hp 15 each (2d8+2)
Fort +0, **Ref** +5, **Will** +2
Defensive Abilities evasion

OFFENSE
Speed 30 ft.
Melee mwk short sword +4 (1d6+2/19–20)
Range dagger +3 (1d4+2/19–20)
Special Attacks sneak attack +1d6

TACTICS
Before Combat If the PCs approach the lookout, he uses Bluff to try passing himself off as a member of the town guard, explaining that he and his comrades are escorting a belligerent youth home.

INTRODUCTION

CHAPTER 1:
THE DELUGE

CHAPTER 2:
BEYOND THE COLONY

CHAPTER 3:
THE SKY TEMPEST TEMPLE

APPENDIX 1:
PRIDON'S HEARTH

APPENDIX 2:
BESTIARY

During Combat If the lookout can see that his ruse isn't working, he throws a thunderstone at the PCs to try to deafen them and warn the other thugs. One of the agents restraining Kanjo moves to assist the lookout, while the remaining thug begins attacking the young man.

Morale If the thugs manage to kill Kanjo, they immediately attempt to flee. They surrender if more than one of them is reduced to fewer than 5 hit points, hoping to escape later.

STATISTICS

Str 14, **Dex** 15, **Con** 10, **Int** 12, **Wis** 10, **Cha** 13

Base Atk +1; **CMB** +3; **CMD** 15

Feats Improved Initiative, Iron Will

Skills Acrobatics +6, Bluff +6, Disguise +5, Escape Artist +6, Intimidate +6, Knowledge (local) +6, Perception +5, Sense Motive +5, Sleight of Hand +5, Stealth +6, Swim +6

Languages Common, Dwarven

SQ rogue talent (fast stealth), trapfinding +1

Combat Gear *potion of cure light wounds*, alchemist's fire (2), thunderstone; **Other Gear** mwk chain shirt, daggers (3), mwk short sword, forged guard badge, 64 gp

---

KANJO ARRAM CR 1/2

XP 135

Human acolyte (*Pathfinder RPG NPC Codex* 244)

hp 5

Development: Searching any of the thugs finds a sketch of Kanjo and a note that says, "Make it look like he left town." Kanjo is terrified, but either Sheriff Adaela or Banker Sifreth can offer him protection for now. Nothing in this encounter directly implicates the Aspis Consortium or Hamsa Gadd, and Sheriff Adaela needs far more evidence than even the testimony of captured goons to arrest one of the count's close friends.

If the PCs are instead working for the Consortium, eliminating Kanjo proves to Hamsa they can be trusted, though her new assistant, Mr. Blackwell, remains

The Serpent Strikes (CR 6)

Eventually, the PCs prove themselves too difficult to control and too big a threat to Aspis operations for Hamsa Gadd to continue tolerating their presence. This encounter occurs anytime after the PCs save Kanjo Arram from the Aspis Consortium (see above). The PCs may initiate it when they go to question Hamsa Gadd about the attack, or Hamsa may decide

to eliminate the PCs once they cross her. This encounter could instead occur when the PCs discover the remains of the Aspis Camp (area **L**) and realize the expedition was wiped out by Mireborn lizardfolk rather than Song'o halflings, proving Hamsa had foreknowledge of the encroaching lizardfolk that could have saved lives during the earlier storm. Charismatic to the end, she apologizes for needing to remove the PCs as players in regional affairs, and promises to send a lovely eulogy to their families describing their untimely deaths due to "local disease."

If the PCs instead work for the Aspis Consortium, Mr. Blackwell sends them a message to meet him after dark. He explains plainly that the Consortium is impressed by their commitment to success, but has found the failure of Hamsa's expedition to be too great a loss to tolerate. If the PCs eliminate her, he offers them as the status of Bronze agents and Hamsa's role controlling Aspis operations in Pridon's Hearth and the Korir River Delta.

Creatures: Hamsa Gadd accompanied the original colonial effort to claim the Korir River Delta 5 years ago, and has carefully groomed the young count into near-total dependence on her advice by subtly questioning the sanity of his decisions and occasionally sabotaging his more willful defiances. She considers the Korir River Delta hers alone to exploit—especially whatever treasures or secrets lie in the Sky Tempest Temple—and she has worked too hard to let anyone take that from her.

Two of Hamsa's agents remain loyal and fight by her side.

HAMSA GADD

HAMSA GADD CR 5

XP 1,600

Female human bard 4/rogue 2

NE Medium humanoid (human)

Init +7; **Senses** Perception +6

DEFENSE

AC 20, touch 15, flat-footed 16 (+4 armor, +1 deflection, +3 Dex, +1 dodge, +1 shield)

hp 41 (6d8+10)

Fort +4, **Ref** +10, **Will** +3; +4 vs. bardic performance, language-dependent, and sonic

Defensive Abilities evasion

OFFENSE

Speed 30 ft.

Melee *+1 corrosive rapier* +7 (1d6+2/18–20 plus 1d6 acid)

Ranged shortbow +7 (1d6/×3)

Special Attacks bardic performance 14 rounds/day (countersong, distraction, fascinate [DC 16], inspire competence +2, inspire courage +1), sneak attack +1d6

Bard Spells Known (CL 4th; concentration +8)

2nd (2/day)—*blur, suggestion* (DC 16)

1st (4/day)—*charm person* (DC 15), *cure light wounds,*
hideous laughter (DC 15), *vanish*^APG (DC 15)

0 (at will)—*light, message, open/close* (DC 14),
prestidigitation, read magic, resistance

TACTICS

Before Combat Hamsa hopes to keep the PCs talking while
her agents quietly slip into position behind them.

During Combat Hamsa begins combat by casting *blur*, then
begins to inspire courage in her allies. She casts *suggestion*
on an easily swayed opponent with, ordering her target to
"defend her from these betrayers," before finally closing in
with her rapier.

Morale Hamsa has sacrificed too much over the past 5 years
to surrender it all now. She fights to the death.

STATISTICS

Str 13, **Dex** 16, **Con** 12, **Int** 10, **Wis** 8, **Cha** 18

Base Atk +4; **CMB** +5; **CMD** 20

Feats Dodge, Great Fortitude, Improved Initiative, Mobility,
Weapon Finesse

Skills Acrobatics +11, Bluff +13, Intimidate +11, Knowledge
(dungeoneering) +9, Knowledge (geography) +7,
Knowledge (history) +7, Linguistics +5, Perception +6,
Perform (oratory) +13, Spellcraft +8, Stealth +10

Languages Common, Halfling, Polyglot

SQ bardic knowledge +2, rogue talent (finesse rogue),
trapfinding +1, versatile performance (oratory)

Combat Gear *potion of cure moderate wounds* (2);
Other Gear *+1 studded leather*, buckler, *+1 corrosive*
rapier, shortbow with 20 arrows, *headband of alluring*
charisma +2, ring of protection +1, explorations journal,
jade earrings (worth 25 gp), 56 gp

SPECIAL ABILITIES

Sign of Station (Ex) Hamsa Gadd carries a *+1 corrosive rapier*
as a sign of her authority within the Aspis Consortium. This
is in addition to her normal wealth for her level, but does
not affect her overall challenge rating.

ASPIS THUGS (2)	CR 1

XP 400 each

hp 15 each (see page 32)

Development: Hamsa Gadd's journal includes many
observations about her failed expedition, including her
account detailing the assault by the Mireborn lizardfolk
and the camp's exact location. Her book also contains
some information about the location of the Sky Tempest
Temple, recalled from memory after she fled her camp
and all her charts. This offers only a general location, and
lacks enough detail to find the temple using the journal
alone. To find the temple's exact location, the PCs need to
find the maps at the old lizardfolk camp in the Ghol-Gan
ruin (see area **B**).

If Hamsa Gadd is slain, Mr. Blackwell and the Aspis
Consortium remain in Pridon's Hearth, but retire into
the background for the next several months and do not
interfere with the PCs' mission to confront the lizardfolk
and save the colony. While excising this cancer from the
community may become the goal for future adventures,
doing so is beyond the scope of this module.

Story Award: If the PCs learn the general location of
the Sky Tempest Temple—either here or from Achahut—
award them an extra 1,600 XP.

I. CAHSHIL (CR 5)

A group of Song'o halflings settled the region just a few
years before the Pridon's Hearth colonists arrived, after
being driven south by the escalating warfare between the
lizardfolk and the boggards in the Laughing Jungle. The
halflings of Cahshil are reclusive and shy subsistence
hunters, and rarely trust or trade with outsiders, leading
to many rumors about them in the absence of hard facts.
Townspeople claim the halflings command terrible
spirits, steal from the farms, and eat human flesh, but
ultimately only one of these rumors contains of kernel
of truth (see area **J**).

The settlement is built upon a particularly deep wetland,
and the halflings construct all their huts atop bamboo
stilts. If the PCs approach with Muhdzuzi or the Song'o
hunters, they find the halflings cautious but welcoming.
Otherwise, the village seems recently abandoned, as the
residents hide nearby to watch the intruders. Eventually,
the Song'o elder Zaahku approaches the PCs flanked by
several warriors, demanding to know why strangers are
bothering her people.

CAHSHIL

CN hamlet

Corruption –2; **Crime** –2; **Economy** –2; **Law** –1; **Lore** –1;
Society –2

Qualities insular

Danger –5

DEMOGRAPHICS

Government autocracy

Population 43 halflings

Notable NPCs

Tribal Elder Zaahku (CN female halfling sorcerer 4)

MARKETPLACE

Base Value 200 gp; **Purchase Limit** 1,000 gp; **Spellcasting** 2nd
Minor Items 1d6; **Medium Items** —; **Major Items** —

Creatures: Zaahku is a concerned leader who errs on
the side of caution. She originally guided her people to
this new settlement years ago. Like her father, she wields
natural magical ability, giving her considerably more
confidence when staring down these stranger outsiders,
and she doesn't hesitate to display her magic if the PCs
become hostile or threatening.

Five Song'o warriors accompany Zaahku, while the rest
of the tribespeople watch from the safety of the trees.

INTRODUCTION

CHAPTER 1:
THE DELUGE

CHAPTER 2:
BEYOND THE COLONY

CHAPTER 3:
THE SKY TEMPEST TEMPLE

APPENDIX 1:
PRIDON'S HEARTH

APPENDIX 2:
BESTIARY

ZAAHKU — CR 3

XP 800

Female halfling sorcerer 4

CN Small humanoid (halfling)

Init +3; **Senses** Perception +4

DEFENSE

AC 18, touch 14, flat-footed 15 (+4 armor, +3 Dex, +1 size)

hp 28 (4d6+12)

Fort +5, **Ref** +8, **Will** +7; +2 vs. fear

Resist cold 10

OFFENSE

Speed 20 ft.

Melee spear +1 (1d6–2/×3)

Bloodline Spell-Like Abilities (CL 4th; concentration +7)

6/day—elemental ray (1d6+2 cold)

Sorcerer Spells Known (CL 4th; concentration +7)

2nd (4/day)—*mirror image*

1st (7/day)—*burning hands* (DC 15), *hydraulic push*^APG, *hypnotism* (DC 14), *mage armor*

0 (at will)—*light, mage hand, message, prestidigitation, ray of frost, read magic*

Bloodline elemental (water)

TACTICS

Before Combat Zaahku casts *mage armor* when scouts first warn her of visitors, and casts *message* on her warriors to help coordinate them in case of attack.

During Combat Zaahku is conservative in combat, using *mirror image* to protect herself and *hypnotism* to distract enemies. If intruders slay one of her guards, she switches tactics, relying on her elemental ray and *burning hands*.

Morale Zaahku hopes to delay dangerous opponents while her people flee, and retreats after 5 rounds. If the PCs kill two or more of her guards, she fights to the death.

Base Statistics Without *mage armor* cast, Zaahku's AC is 14.

STATISTICS

Str 6, **Dex** 16, **Con** 14, **Int** 10, **Wis** 12, **Cha** 17

Base Atk +2; **CMB** –1; **CMD** 12

Feats Eschew Materials, Lightning Reflexes, Scribe Scroll

Skills Acrobatics +5 (+1 when jumping), Climb +0, Diplomacy +4, Intimidate +7, Knowledge (nature) +1, Knowledge (planes) +4, Perception +4, Spellcraft +5, Use Magic Device +7; **Racial Modifiers** +2 Acrobatics, +2 Climb, +2 Perception

Languages Common, Halfling

SQ bloodline arcana

Combat Gear *potion of barkskin* (CL 3rd), *potion of cure light wounds, scroll of mirror image, wand of cat's grace* (8 charges); **Other Gear** spear, *cloak of resistance +1*, flint and steel, sunrods (5), waterskin, Song'o necklaces (worth 60 gp total), 82 sp

SONG'O WARRIORS (5) — CR 1/2

XP 200 each

Halfling expert 1/warrior 1 (use Muhdzuzi's statistics on page 12)

hp 13 each

Development: Zaahku is grateful to anyone who returns Muhdzuzi safely (which completes the Muhdzuzi's Escort quest—see page 21), but ultimately she refuses to trust outsiders. The Cahshil people and many other Song'o tribes have heard promises and bargains from outsiders for decades that invariably work out terribly for the halflings. She steadfastly refuses to involve the tribe in outsider politics. The encroaching storm may threaten them for now, but ultimately the Song'o have survived alongside the Mireborn for centuries. She thanks the PCs if they return one of her people—and offers whatever payment Muhdzuzi promised—but won't be swayed by arguments of passion or pleas for aid.

Zaahku is willing to offer assistance or answer questions only if the PCs offer concrete help to the Song'o first, so she knows they personally are good, trustworthy people. If they agree, she speaks of a tojanida—a strange outsider aligned with the element of water—who lives upriver beneath a grand waterfall (area J). While the Song'o occasionally benefit from the capricious creature's insights and lore, the bullying brute exacted high tolls from them when they first settled in the area. The tojanida, calling herself Guughwa, claimed the tribe's *cauldron of brewing* (*Ultimate Equipment* 287) as a trophy in exchange for letting the halflings settle in "her" river. Zaahku prefers that the PCs don't kill Guughwa—a large monster living so close keeps more aggressive river predators at bay—but she wants the cauldron back and fears to confront Guughwa herself, as the outsider's mood swings can be dangerous. If the PCs succeed at a DC 18 Diplomacy check (or DC 13 if they escorted Muhdzuzi back), Zaahku also lets slip that the tojanida adores coral capuchin eggs, and that a large flock of the creatures nests to the north.

If the PCs return the Song'o *cauldron of brewing*, Zaahku finally accepts them as friends of the tribe and offers them the meager provisions the village managed to put aside. She allows the PCs to rest in Cahshil, and to trade for resources and magic items. At this point she can answer some of the PCs' questions.

Did you attack the Aspis Expedition? "Goodness, no! Our way is to avoid outsiders, not aggravate them. The Mireborn returned to the area unexpectedly, and fell upon your friends without mercy. A few of our hunters looked on, but could hardly have turned the tide either way. They said one woman in orange and green escaped, and a handsome young tallfolk began to parlay with the Mireborn's shaman."

Do you know anything about the Fort Breakthrough attack? "There was an attack? My people generally avoid the region around the outsider fortress. Their tromping and drinking frighten away game."

Who are the Mireborn? "They are our closest neighbors in the area— lizardfolk. They come to the region now and then to fish and bury their dead, but haven't journeyed this far south in quite some time. They're territorial and stubborn, but until this year were always willing to trade. My scouts say they recently lost their territory to a boggard tribe north of the river, and were licking their wounds... probably why they so angrily wiped out your friend's camp near one of their old winter sites."

Do you know anything about this strange weather? "All I know is that this storm is grossly unnatural. Its presence angers Gozreh; it stings like a personal insult. There's little doubt in my mind it has something to do with the expedition the Mireborn attacked, mucking about in those dreadful old Storm Kindler ruins."

Who are the Storm Kindlers?: "My grandfather used to tell scary stories of the Storm Kindlers who arrived in the delta when he was still a child—some sort of Gozreh cult as he recalled, but selfish and rude and arrogant. He claims they bred storms like other tallfolk breed dogs. They built a small village nearby, and later constructed a temple in the Jungle of Hungry Trees. The entire cult vanished in an enormous storm before my grandfather had grown his first whisker, though, and I have upheld his order to let the ruin rest in peace, wherever it may be..."

Zaahku knows little else about recent events, preferring to learn only enough about outside dangers to avoid them or move her people when necessary. The Song'o worship Gozreh, but they consider the Storm Kindlers heretical and dangerous. She doesn't know the location of the Sky Tempest Temple, and takes great pains to keep the rest of her people from seeking it out, or recording its location if they stumble across it, but she can direct the PCs to the Storm Kindlers' village (see area **D**).

Treasure: If the PCs prove themselves friends of the Song'o, Zaahku gifts them her *scroll of mirror image* and *wand of cat's grace* (8 charges) in gratitude. She also offers them a worn old brass key covered in geometric swirls her grandfather found exploring the ruins of the Storm Kindler village, said to ease the rage of winds (see area **N15**).

Story Award: If the PCs earn the trust of the Song'o tribe, award them 1,600 XP.

J. GUUGHWA'S WATERFALL (CR 5)

Five breathtaking cascades of water tumble over the twenty-foot-high, vegetation-covered cliffs surrounding this pristine pool. A mist clings to the water's surface, thick with the scent of a dozen flowering plants. A pastel rainbow of eggshells litters one side of the pool.

GUUGHWA

This 200-foot-diameter pool is home to Guughwa, the occasional ally and frequent bully of the nearby Song'o village of Cahshil. The waters are clean and pure, and nearly 50 feet deep at the center. A small cave can be seen behind one of the waterfalls with a successful DC 14 Perception check.

The eggshells by the side of the pool come from Guughwa's meals. The tojanida adores eggs—a PC who succeeds at a DC 12 Knowledge (nature) check identifies the eggs of 20 different bird and reptile species in the mess. With a successful DC 13 Knowledge (arcana) or Knowledge (local) check, a PC also identifies the eggshells of coral capuchins—a playful magical beast—which seem to be set aside in a place of honor.

Creature: Guughwa is a hedonistic creature, brought to the Material Plane by the first storm summoned by the Storm Kindlers decades ago. She wandered the region, exploiting the generosity of many local tribes, before discovering this picturesque pool and decided to call it her own for now. Guughwa enjoys attention and hospitality, and has spent a decade demanding both from the Song'o. Characters who play into her ego, praising her with a successful DC 15 Bluff or Perform check, gain a +2 circumstance bonus on all future attempts to influence Guughwa's behavior.

The tojanida is a selfish bully, but not especially evil. She approaches newcomers with demands for songs about her own glory and beauty, and becomes violent only if she's attacked or insulted, or if she catches someone stealing from her.

GUUGHWA	CR 5

XP 1,600
Tojanida (*Pathfinder RPG Bestiary* 3 270)
hp 51

Treasure: In addition to the *cauldron of brewing*, Guughwa has acquired a small hoard of treasure. The stash in the back of her cave includes a masterwork set of banded mail armor, a masterwork warhammer, a *scroll of cure breath of life*, an *oil of make whole*, a *potion of darkvision*, and a ruby-encrusted masterwork harp worth 1,000 gp.

Development: Guughwa has no use for the Song'o *cauldron of brewing*, beyond cooking the occasional meal—

she simply likes owning something others want. If a PC succeeds at a DC 13 Diplomacy check, she agrees to trade the item for any item of equal or greater value. Guughwa adores food, and will trade for strange food items and spices at 10 times their normal value, or she will happily trade the cauldron in exchange for 20 coral capuchin eggs if the PCs mention her collection, even pointing adventurers to the nearby nest (area **F**).

Story Award: If the PCs deal with Guughwa peacefully, award them XP as if they defeated the tojanida in combat.

K. FORT BREAKTHROUGH (ABANDONED)

With the storm encroaching, Pridon's Hearth lacks the resources to restaff Fort Breakthrough, and under the constant battering of the weather, the fort quickly falls into disrepair. The PCs can use the fort as a campsite, but each day they are away, there is a 20% chance a creature decides to make its lair in the old structure (use the Korir Delta Encounters table on page 23). The fort is fully detailed in Chapter 1.

L. RUINED ASPIS CAMP (CR 2)

Shredded canvas and a dozen rotting humanoid bodies mar the pristine beauty of this jungle clearing.

The campsite used by the Aspis expedition while exploring the Sky Tempest Temple is near the river, along the Jungle of Hungry Trees. The Mireborn attacked this campsite, slaughtering almost everyone, when the Aspis expedition fell back from the temple. Hamsa Gadd retreated to the settlement, assuming a complete loss, unaware that both Magdi Kukoyi and his elemental follower survived the raid. Mireborn scouts looted most of the camp, leaving behind only the shredded remains of two tents.

A dozen badly decayed bodies litter the campsite. Several javelins remain as well, identical to those wielded by Reszavass and her Mireborn raiders.

Creature: The Mireborn captured the cleric Magdi Kukoyi—a non-Aspis member of the expedition—and imprisoned him within the Sky Tempest Temple. Magdi's friend, Argil—an elemental creature known as a mamiwa—hid during the raid and now lairs near the campsite, waiting for the cleric to return. It fears the Mireborn, having barely survived when they returned to ransack the camp.

Argil is curious about the PCs, and prods them to see how they react. The mamiwa uses its rain speaker ability to talk to their minds and see if they react superstitiously, speaks with animals to annoy or harry the PCs to see if they react violently, and possesses one of the javelins left behind with its elemental infusion to see if these strangers fight over an apparently magical treasure like the lizardfolk did.

Argil flies away if attacked, or if communication seems to be impossible.

ARGIL	CR 2

XP 600
Mamiwa (see page 63)
hp 19

Treasure: A successful DC 14 Perception check to search the campsite reveals a small stash hidden under one of the fireplace rocks, containing 392 sp, a holy symbol of Gozreh, and a *steadfast gut-stone* (*Ultimate Equipment* 320). If the PCs learn the fate of Magdi from Argil and return the holy symbol and at least 250 sp to Kanjo, they complete the Expedition Investigation quest (see page 21).

Development: If the humans seem safe, Argil approaches and asks if they've seen its friend, Magdi Kukoyi, who was stolen away by lizardfolk. Its starting attitude is neutral, and the creature is tight-lipped, but with a successful DC 15 Diplomacy check, a PC improves Argil's attitude to friendly, and it opens up with more details. Argil relates how it and Magdi came with the expedition, discovering the nearby Sky Tempest Temple. It elaborates as much as it can on the Storm Kindler's hope of discovering a breakaway sect of the Storm Kindler faith that supposedly settled in the area almost a century ago, but Argil was ultimately a tagalong and not privy to many of the cult's secrets. He does know that Magdi is kindhearted and friendly, and would never willingly cause the unnatural storms now threatening the region. The elemental offers to accompany the PCs as a guide. If it does, Argil occasionally uses its infusion ability to possess nonmagical weapons to aid the PCs in battle. It can provide details on how to reach the Sky Tempest Temple, personally guiding them to the Mireborn-occupied site.

Story Award: If the PCs deal with Argil peacefully, award them XP as though they defeated it in combat. If Argil leads the PCs to the Sky Tempest Temple, award them an extra 3,200 XP unless they have already received the extra XP from piecing together the location of the ruin from the information found in areas **B**, **E**, and **H**.

M. SKY TEMPEST TEMPLE

The Jungle of Hungry Trees is dense and humid, and despite the relatively recent abandonment of the Sky Tempest Temple, its location is nearly impossible to find amid the foliage. An explorer could stand 50 feet from the structure and fail to notice it—even among the Song'o, who regularly hunt and trap in the jungle, few have spotted it.

Simply exploring this hex is not enough to uncover the Sky Tempest Temple or the Mireborn encampment. PCs need either a guide in the form of the mamiwa Argil (see area **L**), or else a combination of the maps left by the Mireborn near the Ghol-Gan ruin (see area **B**) and either Achahut's descriptions (see area **E**) or Hamsa Gadd's notes (see area **H**).

The Sky Tempest Temple and its surroundings are detailed in Chapter Three.

CHAPTER 3

The Sky Tempest Temple

Whether via a guide or by uncovering enough clues to locate it, the PCs eventually find their way to the Sky Tempest Temple. Nestled within the Jungle of Hungry Trees and covered in thick vines and other overgrowth, the ruin is difficult to spot until explorers are nearly on top of it—the early Aspis expedition only found it thanks to guidance from the modern Storm Kindler Magdi Kukoyi.

The Mireborn

The Mireborn have hunted in and around the Korir River Delta region for hundreds of years, living mostly in the Laughing Jungle and journeying south only to fish the annual run of bull sharks or to inter their dead in the tar pits. The past year has imposed many changes to their lifestyle.

Many of the Mireborn who now live in the temple ruins side with Daruthek out of fear, expecting the humans to wipe them out. His magic required the sacrifice of four Mireborn children as payment to Hshurha, and they tolerate this gruesome price because they see no other way to survive. Enough lizardfolk support Daruthek or are swayed by his faith that the tribe dares not disobey.

As the PCs explore the upper level of the Sky Tempest Temple, the majority of the lizardfolk (especially those in area **M15**) are reluctant to fight. Many assume the PCs arrived explicitly to wipe them out, just as Daruthek predicted. These lizardfolk are considered indifferent for the purpose of talking them down from violence unless otherwise noted, and the DCs for any Intimidate skill checks against them are reduced by 2.

INTRODUCTION

CHAPTER 1:
THE DELUGE

CHAPTER 2:
BEYOND THE COLONY

CHAPTER 3:
THE SKY TEMPEST TEMPLE

APPENDIX 1:
PRIDON'S HEARTH

APPENDIX 2:
BESTIARY

M. SKY TEMPEST TEMPLE

The exiled Storm Kindlers settled on this site after discovering the mist-filled limestone caverns below and interpreted them as a sign of Gozreh's favor. The original construction of the Sky Tempest Temple included the aboveground stone fortifications—an exaggeration of the typically humble architecture associated with Gozreh— and a stairwell leading to the "Sky Tempest" in the caverns below. As She Who Guides the Wind and Waves demands of her faithful, the temple has no roofs, and the stone walls shelter those inside only from outside aggressors, while still admitting the wind and rain from above.

Natural forces and aggressive plant growth eroded the temple quickly in the years following the death of the Storm Kindlers, collapsing portions to the northeast and southwest. The Mireborn lizardfolk also altered the temple and its grounds, adopting several rooms to their own needs and erecting numerous huts to the west. The eastern section of the temple remains untouched by the lizardfolk, who fear and avoid the spirits who dwell there.

Use the map on the inside front cover of this book for the following locations.

M1. The Approach (CR 4)

A weed-choked clearing opens up in the dense jungle, sheltering a basalt structure overgrown with vines and small trees. A foundation of gray stone stands five feet above the ground and runs a hundred and forty feet on each side. Walls rise fifteen feet from this base, decorated with weathered carvings of a man and woman cavorting in storms and ocean waves. Tangled jungle trees loom to the north, while a swath of thatch huts lie to the west.

A variety of grasses and yams—originally planted by the Storm Kindlers, but long since grown wild—fill this small jungle clearing. The surrounding trees create a virtual ceiling and offer some shelter from the raging storm overhead.

Creatures: Three Mireborn lizardfolk guard the clearing at any given time, keeping away animals and gathering wild yams. If they detect intruders, they attempt to duck into the tall grass and flank enemies using Stealth. Failing that, two guards begin harrying intruders with arrows while the third falls back to alert the village.

MIREBORN LIZARDFOLK (3)	CR 1

XP 400 each
Variant lizardfolk (*Pathfinder RPG Bestiary* 195)
hp 11 each
Melee mwk terbutje +3 (1d8/19–20)
Ranged longbow +1 (1d8/×3)
Other Gear mwk terbutje, longbow, 10 arrows

M2. Entryway (CR 4)

Two solid slabs of dark stone rise up fifteen feet into the air, bordered by the walls of the temple on either side and topped with stone depictions of roiling storm clouds.

The original temple doors were sturdy stone, but lacked even locks. While the collapsed walls now make installing a lock pointless, Daruthek nonetheless reinforced the doors with a magical trap.

Trap: Swamp-Speaker Daruthek placed a warding spell over the entry doorway. Any non-lizardfolk opening the doors here trigger the trap, which creates a strike of lightning and an audible clap of thunder, alerting the nearby Mireborn village to the intrusion.

DOOR WARD TRAP	CR 4

Type magic; **Perception** DC 28; **Disable Device** DC 28
EFFECTS
Trigger location; **Reset** none

MIREBORN LIZARDFOLK

Effect spell effect (*glyph of warding*, 5-ft.-radius blast, 3d8 electricity damage, Reflex DC 16)

M3. Temple Promenade

Imposing walls flank this open promenade on the east and west. Images of great storms and floods cover crumbling plaster of the walls, each of which ascend twenty feet into the air. A stone double door lies to the south, while a larger plaza opens to the north.

This wide path represents what was once the entrance and prayer space to the Sky Tempest Temple. The exiled Storm Kindlers painted the numerous frescos to illustrate their early achievements in storm calling, and protected them from the elements with now-faded magic. A PC who succeeds at a DC 17 Knowledge (nature) or Knowledge (religion) check identifies several allusions to Gozreh depicted in the plaster. If the PC succeeds at this check by 5 or more, she also notices a small eye surrounded by crackling lightning in one corner—the symbol of Hshurha, the evil Duchess of All Winds.

M4. Fountain Plaza (CR 5)

A large, raised basin of green rock sits in the center of the temple's plaza. A thick brownish liquid quivers just beyond the fountain's raised lip. A large stone door blocks entry farther north, its surface covered with two circular indentations. Halls extend east and west.

This fountain basin once caught rainwater to supply the cult, both to drink and for various rituals. Without daily castings of *purify food and drink*, the fountain water has transformed into a rancid slurry of algae, disease, and rotting vegetation.

The door to the north requires two seals in order to access. Daruthek bypasses this requirement thanks to the sponsorship of Chitauli (see page 3); the wraith allows him to come and go as he pleases. Chieftain Shathva (located in area **M17**) possesses one seal, while the other rests in area **M8**, clutched in the skeletal arms of a long-dead Storm Kindler. Placing the seals within the two grooves causes the door to shudder open, revealing area **M18**.

Creatures: A pair of ooze mephits—stragglers from the Elemental Plane of Water drawn to the temple ruins decades ago—dwell in the fountain's muck. They spend much of their day splashing through the rancid water, and occasionally stealing from the Mireborn or playing pranks, but Daruthek considers them too valuable as guardians to allow his people to remove the pests.

The mephits hide within the pool and take turns impersonating the "great spirit of the temple" in a completely unintentional perversion of Gozreh's duality. They speak in gurgling Common, demanding intruders throw tribute of gold into the pool for information. For 20 gp or more, the mephits explain their basic understanding of the temple's purpose of summoning elementally infused storms, insisting the process cannot be stopped and visitors should flee for their lives. If they receive offerings of 100 gp or more, the mephits admit that maybe the storm can be stopped, and describe the seals required to enter the lower level of the temple. They mention the "scaled chieftain" possesses one of the two. If the PCs refuse to offer tribute, one of the mephits uses its *stinking cloud* ability to drive them away with noxious fumes.

With a successful DC 13 Knowledge (planes) check, a PC identifies the "great spirit" for what it really is, but the mephits still try to negotiate and even cut their prices by 25% if exposed. The mephits attack if they feel insulted or snubbed, using their *acid arrow* spell-like ability on enemy spellcasters while enjoying fast healing from the rain. If reduced to 5 hit points or fewer, the mephits flee the temple and do not return.

OOZE MEPHITS (2)	CR 3

XP 800 each

hp 19 each (*Pathfinder RPG Bestiary* 202)

Treasure: The pool contains the assembled wealth of the mephits, mostly stolen from lizardfolk: 199 gp, 124 sp, four citrine gems (worth 75 gp each), and a +1 *light flail*.

M5. Green Faith Shrine

Eight irregularly shaped pillars of rock—each carved with unusual symbols—line the western portion of this chamber. Open doorways lead to the north and south.

The Storm Kindlers erected a set of stones fashioned as homages to previous influential members of the Green Faith—a religious philosophy that many of the Kindlers adhered to in addition to their worship of Gozreh. Each pillar features simple prayers in Druidic dedicated to beasts, breath, decay, flame, stone, trees, waves, and wind. Even those unaffiliated with the Green Faith offered small prayers and tokens as a sign of respect. A PC who succeeds at a DC 18 Knowledge (nature) or Knowledge (religion) identifies the significance of these stones and the benefits they can provide divine spellcasters.

Development: Druids, divine spellcasters in service to the Erastil, Gozreh, or the Green Faith, or those with the Air, Animal, Earth, Fire, Plant, Water, or Weather domains who pray for their spells in front of the stones gain a special boon. They can select one of their prepared spells to receive the benefits of the Empower Spell, Extended Spell, Silent Spell, or Still Spell metamagic feat (increasing the spell's effective level as appropriate). This can be done for only one spell, and only when the caster prepares their spells for the day.

M6. Instruments of Wind (CR 4)

Four thin pairs of pillars rise twenty feet to the top of the chamber's walls. Dozens of red silk cords run between the pairs or flutter as frayed strands in the breeze. Small bangles and chimes hang from the intact ropes, jangling in the wind. Broken bones lie scattered throughout the rooms. A doorway leads to the southwest, while a larger chamber lies to the north.

Many of the temple's occupants sought meaning in the natural rhythms beyond storms, including the nuances of the winds. Chitauli allowed these experiments because the wind chimes also provided him a system of measuring the strength of the storms his rituals summoned. Previous storms damaged the chimes, with only a handful of ropes and chimes remaining over the years. Four human skulls can be seen around the room; a PC who succeeds at a DC 12 Heal check identifies the broken bones as human as well.

Haunt: The chamber is one of the few spiritually active regions of the temple. Those Storm Kindlers most opposed to Chitauli's dark bargains gathered here when they realized what he had done. Chitauli used his magic to transform the room into a deadly maelstrom of lashing cords and flying chimes, slaying his enemies only hours before his own demise. The trauma of their deaths generated a terrible echo, which now imposes their shame and horror upon anyone else who enters this room.

CHIMES OF THE DAMNED	CR 4

XP 1,200

CN haunt (20-ft.-by-40-ft. room)

Caster Level 4th

Notice Perception DC 18 (to notice the intensifying sounds of chimes and quiet prayers to Gozreh for forgiveness)

hp 8; **Trigger** proximity; **Reset** 1 hour

Effect A howling wind and panicked screams echo though the room, culminating in the sounding of a single, massive bell. Any living creature in the room must succeed at a DC 14 Will saving throw or be racked by shame and horror at having unwittingly betrayed Gozreh. This shattered self-image imposes a −4 penalty on all saving throws, as well as on all Wisdom- and Charisma-based skill checks. These effects persist until removed with a *break enchantment* or *remove curse* spell, or until the haunt is permanently destroyed.

Destruction To permanently destroy the haunt, the bones of the murdered Storm Kindlers must either be buried or burned on a pyre, and their accidental betrayal of Gozreh forgiven. This requires reciting various prayers—the PCs must succeed at either a DC 15 Knowledge (religion) check to recall the proper rituals, or a DC 22 Bluff or Diplomacy check to fake it.

Development: A single tattered scrap of parchment lies on the flagstone floor, miraculously surviving 90 years worth of rain and sun. This page is all that remains of the diary of Storm Kindler Vauletik, and is still legible.

Chime of Storm Calling

This rare magical chime once featured prominently in Lirgeni rituals, but fell out of fashion with the nation's destruction.

CHIME OF STORM CALLING	PRICE 6,750 GP
SLOT none	**CL** 5th	**WEIGHT** 1 lb.
AURA faint conjuration and evocation		

This copper chime can be struck as a standard action, producing a cloud of mist around the user equivalent to an *obscuring mist* spell. If struck again before the mist disperses, the user can call down the fury of a storm on a single target within the clouded area, either striking it with a bolt of lightning (3d6 electricity damage, Reflex DC 15 half) or buffeting it with a gust of wind for 1 round, equivalent to the spell *gust of wind*. Either use immediately disperses the cloud of mist and renders the *chime of storm calling* inert for 24 hours. If the *chime of storm calling* is not struck again, the mist disperses after 5 minutes, after which it may be used again to create new banks of mist.

A *chime of storm calling* cannot summon lightning or wind while underground, indoors, or in an arid climate.

CONSTRUCTION REQUIREMENTS	COST 3,375 GP

Craft Wondrous Item, *call lightning*, *gust of wind*, *obscuring mist*

Written in Polyglot, it reads, "Chitauli has betrayed our souls to the Duchess of All Winds, and now we hide like rats in the very home we have built, meeting to determine how we may save our souls from the man we followed into this forsaken jungle. Our spirits are broken and our remaining days, I fear, are too short in number. Gozreh, find it in your infinite fairness to spare our wretched spirits for our hubris and blindness, for I lack the depths of courage to forgive myself."

Treasure: Destroying the haunt causes the remaining chimes to fall to the ground and shatter, except for a single one hanging from a red silk cord, glittering gently and illuminated by spiritual light. The departed spirits of the Storm Kindlers transformed this humble instrument into a *chime of storm calling* (see the sidebar).

M7. Meditation Chamber

Two human-sized stone statues stand in the western corners of this area, their features undefined and smoothed by age. Scattered chunks of stone mar the floor, while larger rooms are visible to the north and to the east.

The Storm Kindlers used this chamber to meditate, clearing their minds to be more attentive to the subtle messages of the natural world. The two statues here once depicted the masculine and feminine avatars of Gozreh, but the soft stone has weathered them badly over the past 90 years and they are now virtually unrecognizable.

M8. Lightning Rod (CR 5)

A sturdy green obelisk rises from the center of this chamber to a height of 40 feet, and a corroded metal pole extends another 20 feet from its pinnacle, connected by interlinking chains to four smaller rods driven into the ground. A skeleton wearing a wooden mask rests at the base of the monument, one arm clutched around one of the smaller rods, and another holding a circular, green stone disk.

The Storm Kindlers believed a lightning rod helped entice storms to a structure, and so their temple included one near the meditation chamber, where initiates might glean wisdom from the erratic arcs of electricity. The skeleton at the base of the rod was Meneshep Anut, one of the Storm Kindlers who uncovered Chitauli's deception and murdered their former leader. In shock after the bloody act, Anut walked to this chamber at the height of the storm and committed suicide by touching the lightning rod as electricity coursed through it.

Creatures: The lightning rod attracts the worst of the storm, including an opportunistic pair of lightning elementals who dwell within the rod itself and luxuriate in each lightning strike. They aggressively defend their chamber, and relish the smell of crackling flesh.

MEDIUM LIGHTNING ELEMENTALS (2)	CR 3

XP 800 each
hp 26 each (*Pathfinder RPG Bestiary 2* 116)

Development: The skeleton's hand clutches one of the jade seals required to open the closed door in **M4**.

Story Award: Award the PCs an additional 1,200 XP for recovering this door seal.

Treasure: The skeleton of Meneshep Anut is still wearing *+1 leather armor*, an *amulet of natural armor +1*, and a *ring of swimming*.

M9. Ascetic Quarters

Partially collapsed walls divide this area into large, private chambers. Tattered sheets of canvas hang from the walls, while random stone and cloth debris litter the floors of these rooms.

These chambers once housed the Storm Kindlers before the construction of the temple's lower levels. The Gozreh worshipers rested on hammocks, most of which are no more than fragile rags.

Treasure: A PC who succeeds at a DC 15 Perception check discovers a *necklace of resistance +2* (which has a market price of 6,000 gp) lodged under a piece of collapsed stone. This unique magic item acts as a *cloak of resistance +2*, but takes up the neck slot rather than the shoulders slot.

M10. Broken Ascetic Quarters (CR 6)

The jungle has overgrown the stonework here, collapsing portions of the northern and eastern walls. Chunks of stone wall lie toppled over, partially covered by the advancing foliage. Scattered bits of garbage—mostly animal bones and ragged scraps of cloth—cover the floor.

Structural damage destroyed this portion of the temple.

Creature: A vicious, animate plant known as a shambling mound makes its home here, feeding on animals that enter the temple to find shelter. The Mireborn give this area a wide berth after two of their number fell it.

The odd electrical affinity of the shambling mound makes it slightly more prone to lightning strikes. At the start of every round there is a 10% chance a bolt of lightning strikes the shambling mound. This deals no damage to the creature, but raises its Constitution score by 1d4 points as per its electric fortitude ability.

SHAMBLING MOUND	CR 6

XP 2,400
hp 67 (*Pathfinder RPG Bestiary* 246)

Treasure: A successful DC 17 Perception check reveals the remains of several lizardfolk and an Aspis explorer, now little more than bones and teeth, as well as two *potions of cure moderate wounds* and a sack containing assorted clay statuettes from around the temple (worth 400 gp).

M11. Midden Room (CR 4)

This chamber is divided by a partition that juts from the western wall, leaving a ten-foot entryway to the lower half of the room. Large mounds of dirt rise from overturned flagstones, and scattered piles of rotting animal fur and broken tools cover the remaining floor. Two long-handled nets lean near the only doorway.

The Mireborn use this room as a trash midden, throwing animal remains and broken tools into the steadily growing pile. Because of this and the loose flagstones, the entire room is considered rough terrain.

Creatures: The refuse here attracts a variety of insects and supports a massive population of jungle centipedes, which the Mireborn harvest using the nets to feed their livestock (see area **M16**) or to make various medicines. The centipedes attack en masse if a living creature enters the southern half of the room.

INTRODUCTION

CHAPTER 1:
THE DELUGE

CHAPTER 2:
BEYOND THE COLONY

CHAPTER 3:
THE SKY TEMPEST TEMPLE

APPENDIX 1:
PRIDON'S HEARTH

APPENDIX 2:
BESTIARY

CENTIPEDE SWARM	CR 4

XP 1,200

hp 31 (*Pathfinder RPG Bestiary* 43)

Treasure: A successful DC 18 Perception check while searching the refuse reveals a battered set of *bracers of armor +2*.

M12. The Fighting Pit (CR 4)

The north side of this chamber has a cracked stone floor. To the south lies a pool of thick mud, in which several rows of web-footed tracks are visible. Torn cloth and leather flags of varying colors decorate the walls, each held in place with a metal spike embedded in the stone.

The Mireborn have a long-held tradition of unarmed combat among tribe members, serving as both recreation and a means of settling disputes. In typical settlements, the Mireborn create elaborate fighting pits where they display flags of previous fighting champions and tribal leaders. The lizardfolk's current accommodations in the Sky Tempest Temple force them to improvise, and they have constructed a simpler mud pit by removing several flagstones in this room to hold their fights.

Creature: Elder Othok, the former Mireborn chief, spends most of his days wallowing in the fighting pit to ease his arthritis. Unlike others of his kind, the elder has no immediate urge to flee or attack outsiders. He finds Daruthek's plans and even presence unsettling, and would rather negotiate with the outsiders. Only his age, reputation, and considerable girth keep him from being exiled alongside Achahut.

Othok speaks in Polyglot, and calls the PCs "mewling yolk suckers," offering them a chance to personally wrestle the reigning champion of the Mireborn fighting pits. If one of the PCs can best him in a bout, he promises them all safe passage to the Mireborn chieftain Shathva (if the PCs have not already met her) and to lend his authority to their words. In addition, Othok offers his champion's belt—a glorious adornment of cerulean and jade, loaded with gaudy knickknacks and flair (which is, in reality, a *belt of giant strength +2*).

A PC must succeed at pinning Othok in order to win the match. Age has slowed his reflexes considerably and limited his skill in wrestling, but it has also afforded him immense size, making him a difficult foe to topple. To even out the imbalance in strength, Othok laughingly allows the PCs to use whatever magical items and spells they feel they need to "ease their disadvantage," and refers to this as "greasing up time." The reigning champ bores of PCs who spend more than 3 rounds on pre-match enhancements and begins breaking rocks on his forehead to psych himself up—granting Othok an Intimidate check as a free action against the PCs.

OTHOK	CR 4

XP 1,200

Male old giant lizardfolk fighter 3 (*Pathfinder RPG Bestiary* 295, 195)

CN Large humanoid (reptilian)

Init +0; **Senses** Perception +2

DEFENSE

AC 17, touch 9, flat-footed 17 (+8 natural, −1 size)

hp 43 (5 HD; 2d8+3d10+18)

Fort +9, **Ref** +1, **Will** +5 (+1 vs. fear)

OFFENSE

Speed 30 ft., swim 15 ft.

Melee bite +7 (1d6+4), 2 claws +7 (1d6+4)

Space 10 ft.; **Reach** 10 ft.

TACTICS

During Combat Othok gives smaller opponents a round to get in close without bothering to attempt any attacks of opportunity. He solely uses combat maneuvers even though his youthful skills have slipped away, only lashing out with claw and fang if his opponents attack with weapons.

Morale If pinned, Othok takes his defeat in good humor—no Mireborn has beaten him since Shathva defeated him years ago to claim the role of chief and he enjoys the fight more than the victory. If opponents attack him maliciously, he fights to the death.

STATISTICS

Str 19, **Dex** 10, **Con** 16, **Int** 8, **Wis** 14, **Cha** 12

Base Atk +4; **CMB** +9; **CMD** 19

Feats Combat Reflexes, Improved Unarmed Strike, Iron Will, Persuasive, Power Attack

Skills Acrobatics +4, Craft (weapons) +3, Diplomacy +3, Handle Animal +5, Heal +6, Intimidate +7, Survival +6, Swim +12; **Racial Modifiers** +4 Acrobatics

Languages Polyglot

SQ armor training 1, hold breath

Other Gear *belt of giant strength +2*

SPECIAL ABILITIES

Old (Ex) Othok's advanced age modifies all of his ability scores, and reduces his CR by 1.

Development: A PC who successfully beats Othok in the wrestling match earns the elder's respect and his champion belt. Whether the PCs actually defeat him or not, Othok offers to escort them to Chieftain Shathva and establish a dialogue between the two. Othok is eager to see Daruthek's influence end, mostly out of concern for his tribe and a previous quarrel with the swamp-speaker—Daruthek once attempted to seize the champion's belt rather than win it.

Othok escorts the PCs to area **M17** and speaks with Chieftain Shathva, doing his best to convince the leader of the Mireborn to disassociate the remainder of the tribe from Daruthek's mad invocations. The champion's support grants the PCs a +5 circumstance bonus on all Diplomacy and Intimidate checks to convince the Mireborn to abandon Daruthek and his cult.

Story Award: If a character defeats Othok in a wrestling match, award the PCs 1,200 XP as if they defeated him in combat. The PCs still earn 800 XP for sparring with the elder Mireborn if no one succeeds at pinning him.

M13. Alchemist Hut (CR 5)

The acidic tang of alchemical solvents wafts out from under a canopy, where tables and shelves are lined with all variety of bottles, jars, and dripping bags. Dozens of small cages house various rodents, reptiles, and large insects.

This lab belongs to Croaguhnka, a boggard traitor who fled to the Sky Tempest Temple alongside the Mireborn. Croaguhnka milks the various poisonous creatures for use as alchemical components.

Creature: Croaguhnka spends all her time here, isolated from the Mireborn who still don't trust her. She obsesses over alchemy and despises petty politics, which led to her initial exile. Desperate for a home and support, she offered to construct alchemical traps and smokescreens to cover the Mireborn retreat in exchange for protection.

The boggard alchemist hates outsiders, seeing most creatures as enemies. She attacks quickly, hoping to escape and warn other Mireborn, who can handle the situation.

CROAGUHNKA	CR 5

XP 1,600

Female boggard alchemist 4 (*Pathfinder RPG Bestiary* 37, *Pathfinder RPG Advanced Player's Guide* 26)

NE Medium humanoid (boggard)

Init +1; **Senses** darkvision 60 ft., low-light vision; Perception +5

DEFENSE

AC 18, touch 11, flat-footed 17 (+2 armor, +1 Dex, +5 natural)

hp 77 (7d8+46)

Fort +12, **Ref** +6, **Will** +5; +2 bonus vs. poison

Resist poison resistance

OFFENSE

Speed 20 ft., swim 30 ft.

Melee mwk morningstar +8 (1d8+2) or
tongue +2 touch (sticky tongue)

Ranged acid bomb +7 (2d6+4 acid or fire)

Special Attacks bomb 8/day (2d6+4 fire, DC 16), sticky tongue, terrifying croak

Alchemist Extracts Prepared (CL 4th; concentration +6)
2nd—*blur*, *fox's cunning*
1st—*bomber's eye*^APG, *cure light wounds*, *touch of the sea*^APG (DC 15), *true strike*

TACTICS

Before Combat If Croaguhnka hears intruders—such as the sound of combat in adjoining areas—she drinks her Constitution-enhancing mutagen and extract of *fox's cunning*, then waddles off to investigate.

During Combat The boggard alchemist tosses acid bombs every round, attempting to catch as many enemies as she can in the splash. She uses her *bomber's eye* and *true strike* extracts to improve her throwing capabilities if given an opportunity

Morale Croaguhnka is paranoid of losing her last refuge, and fights to the death.

Base Statistics Without her *fox's cunning* extract and mutagen, Croaguhnka statistics are **AC** 16, **hp** 63; **Fort** +10; **Con** 17, **Int** 14; **Skills** Craft (alchemy) +12, Knowledge (nature) +12, Spellcraft +10, Use Magic Device +9.

STATISTICS

Str 14, **Dex** 12, **Con** 21, **Int** 18, **Wis** 12, **Cha** 6

Base Atk +5; **CMB** +7; **CMD** 18

Feats Brew Potion, Extra Bombs^APG, Iron Will, Point-Blank Shot, Throw Anything, Toughness

Skills Acrobatics +1 (+13 when jumping), Craft (alchemy) +14 (+18 to create alchemical items), Handle Animal +3, Heal +6, Knowledge (nature) +14, Perception +5, Spellcraft +12, Stealth +2 (+10 in swamps), Survival +9, Swim +10, Use Magic Device +8; **Racial Modifiers** +4 Perception, +8 Stealth in swamps

Languages Boggard, Halfling, Polyglot

SQ alchemy (alchemy crafting +4), discoveries (acid bomb, extend potion), hold breath, mutagen (+4/−2, +2 natural armor, 40 minutes), poison use, swamp stride, swift alchemy

Combat Gear *potions of bull's strength* (2), *potions of cure light wounds* (4), *potion of fox's cunning*, *potion of heroism*, *potion of magic fang*, acid (4), twitch tonic^UE; **Other Gear** leather armor, mwk morningstar, *preserving flask*^UE (1st level, *touch of the sea*), mithral cauldron^UE, formula book^UE, tindertwigs (10), 71 gp

Treasure: Croaguhnka's alchemist lab is as valuable as any other. A hanging sack contains his remaining wealth: 106 gp and a *potion of cure serious wounds*. The alchemist's collection of animals is worth 1,000 gp to other alchemists (such as Heri back in Pridon's Hearth), but keeping the collection alive requires a successful DC 25 Handle Animal or Knowledge (nature) check every 24 hours, with the collection losing 100 gp of value for every point by which this check fails as animals grow sick or die off.

M14. Prison (CR 3)

A metal cage fills the southern end of this stone-walled room. A patch of damp hay rests within the cage, along with a bucket and a clay tray covered with the remnants of foodstuffs.

This room was converted into a makeshift prison by the Mireborn, to house their sole prisoner: the second-

CROAGUHNKA

INTRODUCTION

CHAPTER 1:
THE DELUGE

CHAPTER 2:
BEYOND THE COLONY

CHAPTER 3:
THE SKY TEMPEST TEMPLE

APPENDIX 1:
PRIDON'S HEARTH

APPENDIX 2:
BESTIARY

generation Storm Kindler, Magdi Kukoyi. A sturdy padlock and chain (Disable Device DC 25) holds the cage shut. Mireborn guards spend rotating shifts in this chamber, just outside the cell of Magdi. Several overturned wooden buckets serve as impromptu chairs for the guards.

Creatures: A pair of Mireborn guard this chamber, though there is a 75% chance at any given time that one or both guards are dozing on their bucket chairs. A hoop with two keys—one to Magdi Kukoyi's cell and one to his restraints—dangles from a guard's belt. The Mireborn are light sleepers thanks to the warm weather, taking only a –5 penalty on Perception checks to notice intruders.

Magdi Kukoyi is currently locked into a makeshift restraint made from manacles and a breastplate. The odd arrangement prevents the cleric from sleeping soundly, imposing the fatigued condition and consequently keeping him from regaining his spells. The Storm Kindler reacts eagerly to the PCs' arrival, mouthing silent pleas for help. Once the breastplate is removed, Magdi still needs to meditate for spells and sleep to remove his fatigue.

MAGDI KUKOYI

MAGDI KUKOYI	CR 2

XP 800
N cultist (*Pathfinder RPG GameMastery Guide* 278)
hp 16
Domain Spell-Like Abilities (CL 3rd; concentration +5)
  5/day—*icicle* (1d6+1 cold)
Druid Spells Prepared (CL 3rd; concentration +5)
  2nd—*cure moderate wounds, fog cloud*[D], *hold person* (DC 14)
  1st—*endure elements, entropic shield, obscuring mist*[D],
    summon monster I
  0 (at will)—*create water, light, purify food and drink*
    (DC 13), *resistance*
  D domain spell; **Domains** Air, Water

MIREBORN LIZARDFOLK (2)	CR 1

XP 400 each
hp 11 each (see page 39)

Development: Magdi believes any story the PCs tell him when rescued. The Storm Kindler relates his affiliation with a new sect of the order, and how the Sky Tempest Temple belonged to a heretical cell of first-generation Storm Kindlers. If Argil (see area **L**) accompanied the PCs, this immediately improves Magdi's mood, as the cleric reconnects with his lost friend.

Magdi recounts his time with the Aspis expedition and discovering temple. He uncovered heretical prayers to the elemental lords used in the creation of a powerful

ritual, but was unable to gain access to the chambers beneath the temples. The growing tempest leads Magdi to believe that the Mireborn's swamp-speaker perfected the ritual. The cleric offers to accompany the PCs, but suggests dealing with the Mireborn's leader, Chieftain Shathva, first—one way or another.

Story Award: Reward PCs who save Magdi from his imprisonment with an additional 1,200 XP.

M15. Mireborn Village (CR 6)

Huts stand along the western edge of the temple ruins and alongside a lazy river, forming a small village.

The Mireborn are still in the midst of constructing their new shelters at the temple. The area now houses the remainder of the Mireborn tribe, though many of the lizardfolk still roam the nearby jungles in small hunting parties.

Creatures: Many of the remaining 50 Mireborn are either not warriors, still injured from their war, or too young to fight. Most of the population flees into the jungle or river if strangers invade their village. Many of the tribe's remaining warriors spend their time hunting and patrolling the nearby jungles. A contingent of four guards remains behind to protect their people, aided by a pair of trained monitor lizards.

The lizardfolk aren't eager to die defending the temple, especially after seeing Daruthek sacrifice several of their young to enact his ritual. If the PCs announce themselves or aren't immediately aggressive, the lizardfolk demand in broken Polyglot that they stand down and come to speak with Chieftain Shathva.

MIREBORN LIZARDFOLK (4)	CR 1

XP 400 each
hp 11 each (see page 39)

MONITOR LIZARDS (2)	CR 2

XP 600 each
hp 22 each (*Pathfinder RPG Bestiary* 194)

Treasure: Looting the dozen or so huts requires 3 hours of searching (assuming no resistance), and uncovers a hoard of 1,923 gp, 23,403 sp, eight *potions of cure light wounds*, three *potions of barkskin* (1st level), a *scroll of haste*, a *scroll of air walk*, and an *amulet of natural armor +1*.

Development: If the PCs agree to speak with the chief, the Mireborn demand they must be escorted. As a martially inclined culture, the Mireborn don't ask the PCs to put down their weapons, but at least 10 of their number accompany the PCs to the chieftain's hut in area **M17**.

M16. Animal Pen (CR 3)

Gnawed bones, vegetal matter, offal, and an overturned crate fill a makeshift animal pen.

The Mireborn are attempting to rear obedient pets.

Creatures: Three shocker lizards reside in the pens. The unruly creatures have thus far ignored any attempts to train or befriend them. The storm and lightning strikes only worsen the creatures' moods, and they scurry to attack anyone entering their pen or opening the gate.

SHOCKER LIZARDS (3)	CR 2

XP 600 each

hp 19 each (*Pathfinder RPG Bestiary* 248)

M17. Shathva's Hut (CR 6)

The entrance of a large hut faces the ruined walls of the southwestern portion of the temple grounds. Warm furs and stained scraps of fabric line the floor inside the hut, and a burning brazier in its center provides light.

These three conjoined huts serve as the tribe's meetinghouse as well as personal quarters for Shathva and her husbands. Those brought to speak with the chieftain sit on the floor of the central hut, while Shathva sits on an elevated wooden bench.

Creatures: Chieftain Shathva leads the Mireborn by right of might, after challenging and defeating the previous chief, Othok, in single combat; her control now dwindles in the face of Swamp-Speaker Daruthek's growing influence and magical power. Shathva trusts the mutant lizardfolk, having been children together, and feels his plan may now be the only way to ensure Mireborn dominance in this new land. However, she was unprepared for the sacrifices Daruthek's ritual required and grows increasingly restless as the weather worsens. She wallows in her hut, bellowing about her frustrations to her two husbands. Her mates—both handsome paragons among the tribe—console Shathva, but the chieftain continues to flounder in self-doubt over what dark ends Daruthek may be dragging the tribe toward.

Shathva and her husbands are hostile if strangers entire her hut unannounced, bellowing in rage before descending on intruders. However, if guards (from area **M15**) or Elder Othok (from area **M12**) announce the PCs, the Mireborn chief skeptically opens negotiations, at least long enough to find out what the humans of Pridon's Hearth are plotting. Convincing Shathva to abandon Daruthek and his mission requires empathy, quick wit, a silver tongue, and some knowledge of the Mireborn or the surrounding area. PCs must succeed at a total of five DC 20 skill checks in any of the following skills: Bluff, Diplomacy, Intimidate, Knowledge (local), Knowledge

(planes), Knowledge (religion), Perform (oratory), or Sense Motive. A single character can attempt a check in a certain skill only once, but multiple characters can succeed on the same skill check. PCs who have killed any Mireborn around the Sky Tempest Temple take a –2 circumstance penalty on any skill checks to sway Shathva's opinion, while those who dealt peacefully with the neighboring Song'o gain a +2 circumstance bonus. If PCs agree to limit the growth of Pridon's Hearth, or offer the lizardfolk some legitimate stake in the colony's future (such as the land deeds Court Narsus gifted them in the beginning of Chapter 2), they gain a +5 circumstance bonus on all skill checks to sway Shathva.

If the PCs fail to accumulate enough successes, Chief Shathva allows them to leave unharmed, to return to the "human tribe" and encourage the colonists to flee the region. If the PCs refuse to leave or attempt to threaten her, Shathva, her husbands, and any Mireborn escorts attack.

SHATHVA	CR 5

XP 1,600

Lizardfolk barbarian (invulnerable rager) 4 (*Pathfinder RPG Bestiary* 195, *Pathfinder RPG Advanced Player's Guide* 79)

CN Medium humanoid (reptilian)

Init –1; **Senses** Perception +8

DEFENSE

AC 16, touch 7, flat-footed 16 (+4 armor, –1 Dex, +5 natural, –2 rage)

hp 75 (6 HD; 2d8+4d12+28)

Fort +13, **Ref** +1, **Will** +6

DR 2/—, 4/lethal; **Resist** extreme endurance

OFFENSE

Speed 40 ft. (30 ft. in armor), swim 15 ft.

Melee *+1 ghost touch greatclub* +11 (1d10+8), bite +5 (1d4+2) or bite +10 (1d4+5), 2 claws +10 (1d4+5)

Ranged javelin +4 (1d6+5)

Special Attacks rage (13 rounds/day), rage powers (intimidating glare, roused anger)

TACTICS

During Combat Shathva immediately enters a rage, attacking the physically strongest enemies while using her intimidating glare rage power to cow ranged attackers and spellcasters. She freely makes use of Power Attack, and focuses her attention on anyone who dares harm her husbands.

Morale Shathva and her husbands fight to the death.

Base Statistics When not raging, Shathva's statistics are **AC** 18, touch 9, flat-footed 18; **hp** 63; **Fort** +11, **Will** +4; **Melee** *+1 ghost touch greatclub* +9 (1d10+5), bite +3 (1d4+1); **Ranged** javelin +4 (1d6+3); **Str** 17, **Con** 16; **CMB** +8; **Skills** Climb +5, Swim +13.

STATISTICS

Str 21, **Dex** 8, **Con** 20, **Int** 10, **Wis** 10, **Cha** 14

Base Atk +5; **CMB** +8; **CMD** 17

Feats Iron Will, Power Attack, Toughness

Skills Acrobatics +1, Climb +7, Intimidate +10, Perception +8,

INTRODUCTION

CHAPTER 1:
THE DELUGE

CHAPTER 2:
BEYOND THE COLONY

CHAPTER 3:
THE SKY TEMPEST TEMPLE

APPENDIX 1:
PRIDON'S HEARTH

APPENDIX 2:
BESTIARY

Sense Motive +6, Survival +5, Swim +15; **Racial Modifiers**
+4 Acrobatics

Languages Polyglot

SQ fast movement, hold breath

Gear mwk hide armor, *+1 ghost touch greatclub*, javelins (4),
cloak of resistance +1, circular jade seal (worth 300 gp)

SHATHVA'S HUSBANDS (2)	CR 2

XP 600 each
Male advanced lizardfolk (*Pathfinder RPG Bestiary* 294, 195)
hp 15 each

Development: Defeating Shathva in combat breaks the
spirit of many of the surviving Mireborn. The warriors
remain near the temple, more dedicated than ever to
Daruthek's cause, but the other Mireborn collect their
young and abandon the temple in search of a new home
deeper in the jungle. If Elder Othok survives, the chief's
murder hardens him against humans, and he takes over
her role and no longer offers a friendly challenge to PCs.

If the PCs instead convince Shathva to abandon
Daruthek's quest, she agrees to order her guards to no
longer bar their passage. She will not abandon the site,
but keeps the lizardfolk in areas **M1–M17**. She cannot
order Daruthek or his cultists to stop at this point—they
answer to a far more sinister power now—nor can she
even open the doors to the lower temple without the
second seal.

Whether the PCs kill Shathva or negotiate with her,
they gain one of the jade seals required to open the closed
door in area **M4**.

Story Award: If the PCs successfully negotiate with
her, award them 2,400 XP as though they defeated
Shathva and her husbands in combat. Award the PCs
an additional 1,200 XP for recovering this door seal.

Treasure: Along with her equipment, Shathva
maintains a small trove of treasure strewn about her
hut. An hour of searching uncovers 1,305 gp in assorted
gems, along with a pair of *boots of elvenkind* acquired from
one of the Storm Kindler corpses found in the temple. If
the PCs successfully negotiate with the chief, she offers
them the boots and her ghost-crushing bludgeon (a *+1
ghost touch greatclub*) to seal the treaty, as well as the *amulet
of natural armor +1* from area **M15** if they offer her tribe
control of any land in or around Pridon's Hearth.

M18. The Chapel (CR 5)

A heavy roof, constructed from a single block of solid
granite, sets this large chamber apart from the rest of the
open temple. Colorful murals cover the walls, depicting various
birds swimming through the sea and fish soaring through the
clouds. An ominous stairwell fills the center of the room, a
dull, churning roar echoing endlessly from somewhere in
its depths. The broken remains of a statue litter the floor.

The Storm Kindlers paid their respects to Gozreh here,
but shortly after Chitauli ordered the heavy roof built, their
effigy of the god shattered. The stairs here lead down to the
completed second level, eventually connecting to area **N1**.

Druidic script accompanies the murals, detailing the
history of the Storm Kindlers of the Sky Tempest Temple.
The history begins with their exile from the distant
Sodden Lands, and goes on to describe their emigration
to the region, their first ritual storm callings, their second
attempts, and the eventual discovery of a successful ritual.
Nothing mentions discovering Chitauli's treachery in
following the elemental lords, as the order had little time
to update the mural before their destruction. Reading
the full mural takes 15 minutes, and requires fluency in

SHATHVA

Druidic or access to magic such as *comprehend languages*. Magdi Kukoyi, if he accompanies the PCs, can relay this information after reading the mural.

Creatures: The spirits of Chitauli's long-dead collaborators still remain in this chamber, manifesting as shadows. These undead emerge from the murals to attack any creature approaching the stairs. The undead recognize Daruthek and his cultists and allow them free passage.

SHADOWS (2)	CR 3

XP 800 each

hp 19 each (*Pathfinder RPG Bestiary* 245)

N. THE STORM ENGINE

The Storm Kindlers discovered this natural cavern housing an underground river and constantly filled with roiling clouds, and saw it as a sign of Gozreh's favor—a sky hidden away from the world, just for them. As Chitauli's loyalties slipped away from Gozreh and toward the elemental lords, however, he restricted access to the tunnels, permitting only his loyal inner circle to join him below. Hidden from sight and wielding elemental magic, they reshaped the natural wonder into the storm engine, a profane device that could enhance and maintain the weather patterns generated in Storm Kindler rituals. The lower level of the temple also served as a hidden place of worship to Hshurha and Kelizandri, elemental lords of air and water, respectively.

The storm engine diverts water from the underground river and infuses it with elemental cold, fire, lightning, and wind to create a churning maelstrom. The constant storm fills the entire lower level with the eerily musical sounds of wind and falling water, imposing a –5 penalty on all hearing-based Perception checks.

Daruthek has convinced several members of the Mireborn of his glorious purpose, converting these lizardfolk into a loyal cult. The most devoted of Daruthek's followers work alongside the corrupted swamp-speaker. These devoted disciples also have unlocked new mysteries from the texts of the lower floor, learning the powers of the elemental lords Hshurha and Kelizandri. Some chambers feature images of these demigods, and Daruthek and any Mireborn within the lower level carry holy symbols of these obscure deities. A PC who succeeds at a DC 15 Knowledge (religion) check identifies these symbols and recalls some basic knowledge of their patrons.

See the inside front cover for a map of the Storm Engine.

The Storm Seeds

Four powerful magical orbs known as *storm seeds* sustain the storm engine: two tethered to the Elemental Plane of Air, and one each to the Elemental Plane of Water and the Elemental Plane of Fire. Similar to *elemental gems*, each fist-sized quartz sphere contains the essence of an elemental, and uses its captive to channel power directly from its respective Elemental Plane. The *storm seeds* are fragile (hardness 1, 10 hp), and if broken, they explode in a cascade of energy that deals 5d6 points of energy damage to any creature within 10 feet (the exact type varies for each orb). Destroying a *storm seed* immediately severs its tether. Shutting down the tether without destroying the *storm seed* requires either a successful DC 20 Use Magic Device check or a successful casting of *dispel magic* (CL 10th). Reactivating a *storm seed* requires ritual magic involving the sacrifice of a sentient being.

The maelstrom created by the orbs forms a powerful barrier of elemental wind and water that completely protects the central platform (area **N19**). This barrier ascends to the roof of the lower level, where the engine's magic channels it high into the sky overhead, preventing any effect from reaching within. Most weapons and spell effects cannot penetrate the barrier. Teleportation and similar spell effects work normally to bypass the barrier, but such effects are likely be beyond the reach of the PCs at their current level.

Destroying the barrier and confronting Daruthek requires destroying or deactivating all four *storm seeds*. Though the storm engine required all four tethers for Daruthek to begin the ritual, it can continue maintaining the barrier in area **N19** and empowering storms for days with only a single *storm seed*—more than enough time to wipe away the town of Pridon's Hearth.

N1. Landing

Hot, moist air and the roar of falling water fill this room. The descending stairs end at a twenty-foot-long hallway, which expands briefly before abruptly opening onto a huge chamber. Torches on the western and eastern walls illuminate the area.

The stairs down from area **M18** end here. Daruthek's cultists keep the floating platform (see area **N2**) tethered here, mostly traversing the complex via *levitation* or flight.

N2. The Maelstrom Chamber

The edge of the corridor falls down twenty feet to a swirling lake that stretches out fifteen feet before coming to a wall of churning storm clouds rising up to the chamber's ceiling. A wedge-shaped plinth hovers twenty feet above the swirling waters, supported by some unseen force and lashed to iron rings in the wall with sturdy-but-damp ropes.

The lake below swirls in a constant whirlpool, and anyone falling into the water from above takes 1d6 points of falling damage, followed by 1d6 points of nonlethal damage each round as they are buffeted by the strong currents. Anyone who loses consciousness in the water is ejected through the subterranean river system, washing ashore near area **M15**, alive but half-drowned.

INTRODUCTION

CHAPTER 1:
THE DELUGE

CHAPTER 2:
BEYOND THE COLONY

CHAPTER 3:
THE SKY TEMPEST TEMPLE

APPENDIX 1:
PRIDON'S HEARTH

APPENDIX 2:
BESTIARY

The platform is a unique magical device constructed by the original Storm Kindlers to traverse their ambitious underground complex. The platform floats thanks to a permanent *levitate* spell effect, and a sail hung below it catches the winds that circle the chamber. When not tethered to the wall here, it floats slowly around the chamber's circumference, pausing for 2 rounds at a time at areas **N1**, **N3**, **N11**, the corridor to **N12**, and **N15**. The platform completes one circuit every 4 minutes.

The barrier in the room's center acts as a *wall of force*, and deals 1d6 points of electricity damage and 1d6 points of cold damage to creatures that touch it.

The entrance at area **N11** is blocked by fallen rubble, but the same quake that collapsed this passage also opened a side cavern just below the waterline (see area **N7**). PCs can spot this opening from the floating platform with a successful 12 Perception check, but reaching it requires either a successful DC 20 Swim check to navigate the turbulent waters or else clever use of ropes or magic.

N3. Northwind Channel (CR 4)

A frigid wind blows constantly from deeper within the complex, gusting snow and mist into the central vortex. Thick sheets of frost line the floor and walls of this chamber. Against the eastern wall stands one statue that depicts a sinewy woman wrapped in flowing, diaphanous shawls, and another that resembles an upright draconic creature with gills. Halls exit to the west, dropping into the lake, and to the east into colder regions.

The northeast portion of the storm engine channels cold from the Elemental Plane of Water. The statues here depict Hshurha and Kelizandri, the elemental lords of air and water, respectively, and this chamber serves as a shrine to the demigods. PCs who succeed at a DC 18 Perception check notice a concealed door behind the ice of the southern wall of the corridor between this area and area **N4**, but opening it requires destroying the sheet of ice covering it (hardness 0, 9 hp).

Creature: Chitauli's first bargains with the elemental lords brought strange and unique servants to aid his efforts, including a rare, cold-infused gelatinous cube vital for regulating the flow of elemental energy through the chamber. The ooze begins trapped by a sheet of ice in an alcove overhead, and is difficult to detect (Perception DC 30), but if the *storm seed* in area **N5** is deactivated or destroyed, the slush cube is released and begins slowly making its way east to the coldest parts of the complex.

SLUSH CUBE	CR 4

XP 1,200

Unique advanced gelatinous cube (*Pathfinder RPG Bestiary* 294, 138)

N Large ooze

Init –2; **Senses** blindsight 60 ft.; **Perception** –2

DEFENSE

AC 9, touch 7, flat-footed 9 (–2 Dex, +2 natural, –1 size)

hp 58 (4d8+40)

Fort +11, **Ref** –1, **Will** –1

Immune cold, electricity, ooze traits

OFFENSE

Speed 15 ft.

Melee slam +4 (1d6+3, plus 1d6 acid and 1d6 cold)

Space 10 ft.; **Reach** 5 ft.

STATISTICS

Str 14, **Dex** 6, **Con** 30, **Int** —, **Wis** 6, **Cha** 6

Base Atk +3; **CMB** +6; **CMD** 14 (can't be tripped)

Skills Acrobatics –2 (–10 when jumping)

SQ engulf, numbing cold, paralysis, transparent

SPECIAL ABILITIES

Numbing Cold (Ex) A slush cube's slam attacks deal 1d6 points of cold damage in addition to its normal acid damage.

Treasure: Small bubbles within the slush cube are actually clear crystals carried from the Elemental Plane of Water. The ooze contains a total of seven such gems, each worth 150 gp.

N4. Prayer Chamber

Thick sheets of ice cover the walls and floor here, formed by the bone-chilling cold that suffuses the room. Two wooden benches stand opposite each other here. Bas-reliefs carved into the icy layer depict a myriad of humans worshiping a vast dragonlike creature while others show devotees venerating a raging cyclone.

Storm Kindlers used this chamber to pray to Hshurha and Kelizandri, finding focus and absolution in the painful cold. The wall carvings depict common images of the elemental lords of air and water.

Hazard: This chamber and area **N5** are areas of severe cold, requiring a successful Fortitude save every 10 minutes to avoid taking 1d6 points of nonlethal damage from the cold (*Pathfinder RPG Core Rulebook* 442). The icy floor counts as difficult terrain.

N5. Convection Room (CR 6)

The hall expands into a larger chamber, curving out until it's thirty feet long and thirty feet wide. A cage of icy shafts encloses a floating, crystalline orb three feet above the stone floor. Two rime-coated statues flank the hallway leading south.

This chamber houses the *storm seed* channeling the frigid depths of the Plane of Water. The icy bars of the cage can be broken with a successful DC 18 Strength check or by 12 points of bludgeoning or slashing damage.

Creatures: Two very unusual creatures guard the *storm seed* here: a pair of aquatic gargoyles known as kapoacinths.

Fanatical followers of Kelizandri, the pair dwelled in the storm engine for years following the original Storm Kindlers' extermination, coming and going via the underground river to hunt. They allied with Daruthek when the lizardfolk arrived, and now guard one of the temple's *storm seeds*, posing as statues to ambush intruders.

KAPOACINTHS (2)   **CR 4**
XP 1,200 each
Variant gargoyle (*Pathfinder RPG Bestiary* 137)
hp 42 each
Speed 40 ft., swim 60 ft.

Hazard: This chamber and area **N4** are areas of severe cold, requiring a successful Fortitude save every 10 minutes to avoid taking 1d6 points of nonlethal damage from the cold (*Pathfinder RPG Core Rulebook* 442). The icy floor counts as difficult terrain. The kapoacinths' claws allow them to treat the icy surfaces as normal terrain.

Treasure: The kapoacinths each wear a *ring of inurement* (see the sidebar on page 51) to protect themselves from the room's chill, and a coral unholy symbol of Kelizandri (worth 100 gp) scavenged from the Storm Kindlers' belongings.

Development: Destroying the *storm seed* here unleashes a blast of cold energy (see page 48). Destroying or deactivating the *storm seed* also releases the slush ooze trapped in area **N3**.

Story Award: If the PCs destroy or deactivate the *storm seed* here, award them an additional 1,200 XP.

N6. Service Passage

This simple tunnel is a remnant of the limestone caverns from which the Storm Kindlers excavated the complex.

N7. Flooded Cavern (CR 5)

The crystal-clear waters here pulse rhythmically through this stalactite-cluttered aquatic cavern. A maelstrom rages outside through the cavern's northwest exit, and occasional flashes of light shine from the southeast end of the passage.

The entry to this cavern from area **N2** lies just below water level and is easily spotted with a successful DC 12 Perception check. This limestone cavern lies completely below water level, having been exposed and flooded in the same small earthquake that collapsed the entrance to the lightning array (area **N11**). The waters in this area are rough, due to the turbulence of the effects outside. Non-aquatic creatures in the area must succeed at DC 13 Swim checks in order to maneuver.

Creatures: Three eels swim around this cavern, having formerly lived and hunted in the larger pool before Daruthek's ritual made it uninhabitable. Their isolation has left them hungry and aggressive, and they rush to attack any prey.

ELECTRIC EELS (3)   **CR 2**
XP 600 each
hp 17 each (*Pathfinder RPG Bestiary* 119)

Treasure: The currents collect a variety of strange things here, including a quiver of six *+1 bolts*, a bottle of Lirgeni coffee liqueur (worth 50 gp), a masterwork silver ocarina (worth 150 gp), a pearl ring (worth 250 gp), and 3,252 sp in Lirgeni coins. A large key also lies on the cavern's floor, and opens the locked chest in area **N14**.

N8. Storm Kindler Archives (CR 4)

The smell of ozone and mildew fills the air of this neglected chamber. Crooked bookshelves crowded with ragged tomes occupy much of the room. The cracked floor slopes toward a large, water-filled passage leading west. To the south stands a sturdy wooden door covered in shallow gouges.

Chitauli moved the Storm Kindlers' library into this vault, separating his flock from the words of Gozreh to help tighten his grip over their beliefs as he began working apocryphal rituals and secrets into their prayers. PCs can discover the secret door in the north wall with a successful DC 18 Perception check.

Creatures: A group of Chitauli's followers barricaded themselves in the vault when the larger cult revolted, and were locked inside. They discovered the secret passage, but couldn't budge the ice sheet sealing the far end. Eventually they resorted to cannibalism, and after finally starving to death, three of their number rose as ghouls. Frustrated with their entrapment, the three undead destroyed most of the library and its contents in multiple tantrums. They briefly explored the flooded passage to the west when it opened 20 years ago, but ran afoul of the kapoacinths dwelling in the central lake and retreated to their den.

The ghouls eventually reconnected with Chitauli's restless spirit, who had the lizardfolk release them. They now serve Daruthek in trying to repair the damage they inflicted over 90 frustrating years of confinement. Still ravenous—they're trying to resist eating the lizardfolk cultists—they attack any humanoids who enter.

GHOULS (3)   **CR 1**
XP 400 each
hp 13 each (*Pathfinder RPG Bestiary* 146)

Treasure: Water and the ghouls' rage destroyed many of the valuable tomes once stored here, but a copy of *Hymns to the Winds and the Waters* constructed with bronze pages survived both the ghouls' wrath and the moisture. The book is worth 500 gp on its own, but also several pages also function as scrolls of the following spells: *barkskin, dispel magic, dominate animal, lightning bolt, restoration,* and *summon nature's ally II.*

N9. Elemental Library (CR 5)

The stale aroma of parchment fills this square chamber. Large wooden bookshelves line the perimeter, each stuffed full of beaten tomes and loose papers. A circular table sits in the center of the room, flanked by two chairs and covered with numerous open texts. A path opens to a larger chamber to the west, while a door allows passage further north.

This area contains much of Chitauli's collected knowledge on the elemental lords and the workings of the storm engine. Some came with the Storm Kindlers during their exodus—primarily cautionary tales—but far more arrived piecemeal, purchased from traders or transcribed by Chitauli deep in the throes of communion with planar forces. Legitimate texts regarding Gozreh were locked in a side chamber (area **N8**); most of the works here are heretical treatises venerating the elemental lords.

A PC who spends time studying here learns much of Chitauli's personal philosophy, desperation, and lust for power, as well as the basic workings of the storm engine and the existence of the Chancel of Four Winds (area **N19**) in the very center of the complex. Spending at least 4 hours studying here allows a character to attempt to deactivate a *storm seed* with the Use Magic Device skill untrained, and provides a +5 insight bonus on skill checks to do so.

Creatures: Three of Daruthek's indoctrinated followers reside here. These nascent clerics of Kelizandri simply emulate their teacher, understanding little of the Brackish Emperor's philosophy but enthralled by the power he provides. Regardless of the PCs' relationship with the Mireborn tribe above, these cultists are loyal only to Daruthek, and attack intruders.

DISCIPLES OF DARK WATER (3)	CR 2

XP 600

Lizardfolk cleric of Kelizandri 2 (*Pathfinder RPG Bestiary* 195)

NE Medium humanoid (reptilian)

Init +0; **Senses** Perception +1

DEFENSE

AC 18, touch 10, flat-footed 18 (+3 armor, +5 natural)

hp 20 (4d8+2)

Fort +6, **Ref** +2, **Will** +4

OFFENSE

Speed 30 ft., swim 15 ft.

Melee mwk trident +6 (1d8+4), bite +0 (1d4+1)

Special Attacks channel negative energy 4/day (DC 12, 1d6), destructive smite (+1, 4/day)

Domain Spell-Like Abilities (CL 2nd; concentration +3)

4/day—*icicle* (1d6+1 cold)

Cleric Spells Prepared (CL 2nd; concentration +3)

1st—*cure light wounds, endure elements, entropic shield, true strike*^{D}

0 (at will)—*bleed* (DC 11), *create water, light, resistance*

D Domain spell; **Domains** Destruction, Water

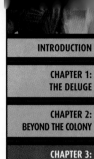

INTRODUCTION

CHAPTER 1:
THE DELUGE

CHAPTER 2:
BEYOND THE COLONY

CHAPTER 3:
THE SKY TEMPEST TEMPLE

APPENDIX 1:
PRIDON'S HEARTH

APPENDIX 2:
BESTIARY

Ring of Inurement

These rings help their wearers survive extreme environs, removing the need for specialized clothing and gear.

RING OF INUREMENT		PRICE 1,000 GP
SLOT ring	**CL** 1st	**WEIGHT** —
AURA faint abjuration		

This humble ring is crafted from smooth red and blue porcelain and wrapped with threads of copper. Each morning, the ring's wearer must select either hot or cold, and for the next 24 hours the *ring of inurement* affords basic protection from the selected condition as if she were using *endure elements* and superficially alters the wearer's clothing to better accommodate her, growing fur linings and extra layers in frigid environs or lightening fabric in response to high temperatures. The ring protects only the wearer who determined its properties for the day, and its protection immediately ends for the day if it is removed.

CONSTRUCTION REQUIREMENTS	COST 500 GP

Forge Ring, *endure elements, prestidigitation*

TACTICS

Before Combat Each morning the disciples cast *endure elements* on themselves to navigate the dungeon's extreme climates. If they hear combat nearby, they cast *entropic shield*.

During Combat Daruthek's disciples attack with destructive smite and tridents or hurl icicles at distant opponents. They use little strategy, pausing to heal themselves only if reduced to fewer than half their hit points.

Morale The disciples fight to the death.

STATISTICS

Str 17, **Dex** 10, **Con** 10, **Int** 12, **Wis** 13, **Cha** 12

Base Atk +2; **CMB** +5; **CMD** 15

Feats Lightning Reflexes, Power Attack

Skills Acrobatics +4, Climb +7, Handle Animal +7, Knowledge (religion) +5, Sense Motive +7, Spellcraft +7, Swim +12; **Racial Modifiers** +4 Acrobatics

Languages Draconic, Polyglot

SQ hold breath

Combat Gear *scroll of spiritual weapon;* **Other Gear** *+1 leather armor*, mwk trident, silver unholy symbol of Kelizandri (worth 25 gp)

Treasure: One of the texts here was a *golem manual*, which Daruthek used to create the ice golem in **N14**. PCs can still identify the book, which hints at the golem's presence, with a successful DC 24 Spellcraft check. Much of the collection is gibberish or commonly available, but PCs can uncover the following rare tomes with a successful DC 18 Appraise or Knowledge (arcana) check: *Rhetorical*

Exploits in Conjuration (worth 150 gp), *Gwidget's Ethnology of the Inner Planes* (worth 90 gp), *Music and the Equatorial Storm Front: A Meteorological Reference* (worth 100 gp), and *Poems to Contemplate While Drowning* (worth 35 gp). In addition, a *trident of stability*[UE] lies on a nearby table; once Chitauli's personal weapon, Daruthek and his minions covet the tool but dare not touch it for fear of angering Chitauli's spirit.

N10. Lightning Array (CR 7)

Arcs of lightning leap between a curious collection of glass and metal devices inside this room. A collapsed tunnel once exited to the northwest, and a door leads east. A small alcove sits in the western wall, in which a fist-sized orb of yellow crystal floats three feet above the ground.

This chamber houses one of the *storm seeds*, channeling a constant flow of electrical energy that helps to fuel the thundering storms outside. An earthquake destroyed much of the delicate equipment here, and now Daruthek relies on the room's incorporeal resident to channel the elemental power into the rest of the storm engine.

Creatures: Chitauli, former leader of the Storm Kindlers, returned as a wraith shortly after his death at the hands of his followers. He guided the Mireborn's spiritual leader—the Swamp-Speaker Daruthek—into recreating the ancient storm ritual that now threatens the entire region, hoping the completion of his life's work will allow him to move on. With this portion of the dungeon damaged, Chitauli himself serves as a conduit for the elemental power produced by the *storm seed*, so slaying the spirit has the same effect as deactivating the *storm seed* in the alcove.

Two air elementals guard the *storm seed* itself, and join the fight only if PCs move towards their charge.

CHITAULI	CR 5
XP 1,600	

Wraith (*Pathfinder RPG Bestiary* 281)
hp 47

MEDIUM AIR ELEMENTALS (2)	CR 3
XP 800 each	

hp 30 each (*Pathfinder RPG Bestiary* 120)

Hazard: The arcing electricity here strikes careless, clumsy, or unlucky visitors, and deals 2d6 points of electricity damage if touched (Reflex DC 15 half). Each time a character in this room rolls a natural 1 on an attack roll or Acrobatics skill check, he connects with one of these power flows. Chitauli is likewise vulnerable to this effect, but as an incorporeal being he takes only half damage on a failed Reflex save and one-quarter damage with a successful save.

Development: Destroying the *storm seed* here unleashes a blast of electricity energy (see page 48).

Story Award: If the PCs destroy or deactivate the *storm seed* here, award them an additional 1,200 XP.

N11. Lightning Array Entry

Shattered bits of glass—and a handful of intact rods—line the walls of this short hall, which ends in a slide of broken rock and dirt.

This hall channeled the dangerous electrical energies of the lightning array directly into the storm engine, insulating the rest of the complex, but an earthquake decades ago collapsed the tunnel. Chitauli's presence (see area **N10**) channels the necessary power from the lightning array into the engine, so Daruthek hasn't bothered to clear the passage. Without magical aid, clearing the passage requires a total of 40 hours of backbreaking labor.

N12. Hothouse Barracks (CR 5)

Rippling waves of heat distort the air in this long room, where ten humble bunks line the walls. A passageway leads east from the north end of the room and south. Currents of hot air constantly blow from the southern corridor and out to the larger complex.

Chitauli's inner circle eventually moved into this sauna-like barrack, disciplining themselves by acclimatizing to extreme heat. So close to the *storm seed* linked to the Elemental Plane of Fire, this room is even warmer than the jungles above. The southern door is barred shut.

Creatures: Two of Daruthek's cultists rest here at any time, praying and training.

DISCIPLES OF DARK WATER (2)	CR 2
XP 600 each	

hp 20 each (see page 51)

Hazard: This chamber is an area of very hot conditions; each creature must succeed at a Fortitude save every hour to avoid taking 1d6 points of nonlethal damage from the heat (as described on page 444 of the *Core Rulebook*).

N13. Furnaces (CR 5)

Sturdy iron doors cover small niches in the eastern wall of this wide chamber, and a variety of tools, metal poles, and crucibles line shelves carved into the western wall. An iron door in the east wall currently stands open. Three emaciated corpses, mummified in the room's oppressive heat, lie on the ground. A hefty iron door seals a passage to the east.

Chitauli's cult used this area to manufacture much of the glass rods and bulbs needed for the lightning array and other components of the storm engine. The various furnace doors against the eastern wall connect to a series of flues and vents connected to the warming chamber (area **N14**), concentrating the heat to high enough temperatures to melt and work glass. The lizardfolk avoid this room for fear of the haunt.

Haunt: When the Sky Tempest Temple fell, the door to area **N12** jammed shut, trapping several Storm Kindlers trapped in here. They died painfully, choking on toxic fumes, and their agonizing deaths formed a haunt.

SUFFOCATING END HAUNT	CR 5

XP 1,600

CE persistent haunt (15-ft.-by-40-ft. room)

Caster Level 6th

Notice Perception DC 20 (to notice the furnace doors rattling)

hp 22; **Weakness** vulnerable to cold damage; **Trigger** proximity; **Reset** 1 day

Effect When this haunt is triggered, the furnace doors burst open, releasing vents of superheated gasses. Any creatures in the room take 2d6 points of nonlethal damage every round from the intense heat and muscle spasms (Fortitude DC 14 half). At the beginning of each round, living creatures in this room must also succeed at a DC 14 Fortitude save or be staggered for 1 round.

Destruction The three dead bodies be laid to rest in fresh water, or a half-gallon of water must be poured down each of their throats.

Hazard: Even when the haunt is not activated, this chamber is an area of very hot conditions; each creature must succeed at a Fortitude save every hour to avoid taking 1d6 points of nonlethal damage from the heat (as described on page 444 of the *Core Rulebook*).

Treasure: Three sets of masterwork glassblowing tools sit on the shelves, as well as 36 high-quality glass decanters (worth 15 gp each). Each decanter contains enough *potion of resist energy (fire)* for two people to imbibe.

N14. Warming Chamber (CR 6)

Charred stone walkways cross over a shallow pool of boiling water in this room's center. A sturdy treasure chest is bolted to the floor in the northeast corner. A red, fist-sized orb floats three feet above the room's center.

This large chamber houses a *storm seed* connected to the Elemental Plane of Fire, transforming the natural pool here into an artificial hot spring.

Creature: Daruthek used a *golem manual* he discovered in the library (area **N9**) to create an ice golem guardian for the *storm seed* here. Despite the high temperatures, the golem's construct nature protects it from the climate, and Daruthek believes himself unreasonably clever for

protecting the dungeon's hottest chamber with a minion made of ice.

ICE GOLEM	CR 5

XP 1,600

hp 53 (*Pathfinder RPG Bestiary* 161)

Hazards: This chamber is an area of extreme heat. Any creature breathing the blistering air takes 1d6 points of fire damage every minute and must succeed at a Fortitude save every 5 minutes to avoid taking 1d4 points of nonlethal damage from the heat (as described on page 444 of the *Core Rulebook*). Additionally, creatures knocked off the walkways into the boiling water in the 2-foot-deep pool 5 feet below take 4d6 points of fire damage each round they remain in the water.

Treasure: A locked chest (Disable Device DC 30) contains a set of two matching wands: one *wand of flame*

INTRODUCTION

CHAPTER 1:
THE DELUGE

CHAPTER 2:
BEYOND THE COLONY

CHAPTER 3:
THE SKY TEMPEST TEMPLE

APPENDIX 1:
PRIDON'S HEARTH

APPENDIX 2:
BESTIARY

CHITAULI

sphere (10 charges) and one *wand of cure moderate wounds* (10 charges). Resting between the two wands is a set of ceremonial robes (worth 500 gp), which conceals a *headband of alluring charisma +2*. The key to this chest was dropped into the central lake when the temple fell, and now lies submerged in area **N7**.

Development: Destroying the *storm seed* here unleashes a blast of fire energy (see page 48).

Story Award If the PCs destroy or deactivate the *storm seed* here, award them an additional 1,200 XP.

N15. Wind Gate (CR 4)

Double doors etched with geometric swirls and curves representing wind stand at the top of a short flight of stairs to the north of this landing. The left door has a small keyhole.

A pair of sturdy double doors block this portion of the dungeon. While the doors aren't locked, opening them without using one of the matching brass keys triggers the trap.

Trap: If the double doors here are opened without using one of the brass keys (the lizardfolk cultists within have one and Zaahku of Cahshil has the other), a magical trap creates a powerful blast of wind to knock intruders back, possibly pushing them into the waters of area **N2**.

REPELLENT WINDS TRAP	CR 4

Xp 1,200
Type magic; **Perception** DC 28; **Disable Device** DC 28
EFFECTS
Trigger touch; **Reset** automatic
Effect spell effect (*hydraulic torrent*, +6 CMB); multiple targets (all targets in 10-ft.-by-20-ft. chamber)

Story Award: If the PCs acquired the old key from Zaahku in the Song'o village of Cahshil (see area **I**), award them 1,200 XP as if they defeated the trap normally.

N16. Apiary (CR 4)

Dull, waxy hives line the walls of this chamber, spilling honey into filthy, insect-laden pools on the floor. Cobwebs fill the space between hives, and a stairway to the west leads up toward the howl of intense winds somewhere beyond.

The cultists kept a large colony of aggressive Mwangi bees here to court Hshurha's favor and guard one of the *storm seeds*, but the rebelling Storm Kindlers killed much of the hive—including the queen—on their way to smash the magic orb. The honey from the decaying hive has attracted all manner of insects and unusually large predators.

Creatures: A trio of giant spiders reside in the tunnels above this chamber, dropping on prey from above and using their webs and poison to immobilize their targets.

GIANT SPIDERS (3)	CR 1

XP 400 each
hp 16 each (*Pathfinder RPG Bestiary* 258)

Development: Uurgu (see area **N17**) casts *alarm* on this chamber each day to warn her of intruders.

Treasure: With a successful DC 20 Perception check, a PC spots a niche hidden behind one leaky, waxen wall, which contains three sealed jars of giant royal jelly (*Pathfinder RPG Bestiary 2* 43, 100 gp each) and a *pearl of power* (3rd level).

N17. Choral Hall (CR 6)

The howling of cyclonic winds fills every corner of this high-ceilinged chamber. A circle of bronze posts stretches up to the roof, forming a cage in the southern end of the chamber. Visible blasts of air move from the cell and south into a series of branching tunnels and strangely fluted walls.

This chamber was both a shrine to Hshurha and an ingenious musical instrument, using the air currents generated by a *storm seed* tied to the howling winds of the Elemental Plane of Air, and funneling them into carefully carved channels to create haunting music.

After the Storm Kindlers discovered Chitauli's betrayal and murdered him, they smashed the *storm seed* stored here in hopes doing so would end the growing hurricane outside. Thanks to the storm engine's design, the anomalous weather continued for days—long enough to destroy the remaining Storm Kindlers. Without the resources to craft a new *storm seed*, Chitauli and Daruthek developed a clever substitute: binding a powerful elemental creature known as a djinni and using her power in its place.

Creatures: Daruthek's trusted apprentice Uurgu guards the magical prison here, and makes frequent adjustments to the ritual binding the genie and harnessing her power. A pair of lizardfolk dark water disciples assist Uurgu in her work.

The djinni is a resident of the Elemental Plane of Air known as Lady Fafrail. With guidance from Chitauli, Daruthek conjured the genie with a unique *planar binding* ritual that imprisoned the outsider and now uses her as a conduit to the elemental energies of the Great Beyond. The process is both painful and degrading, leaving the proud outsider quivering with rage and barely coherent while trapped behind the bronze bars. The prison prevents the Lady Fafrail from moving, attacking, or using any of her spell-like abilities, but destroying any of the brass rods in her magical cage (hardness 10, 10 hp) frees her immediately. If freed, she immediately joins the fight to kill any remaining lizardfolk before recovering her composure.

Lady Fafrail currently has 2 negative levels, thanks to the incredible toll acting as an elemental tether takes on her body.

INTRODUCTION
CHAPTER 1: THE DELUGE
CHAPTER 2: BEYOND THE COLONY
CHAPTER 3: THE SKY TEMPEST TEMPLE
APPENDIX 1: PRIDON'S HEARTH
APPENDIX 2: BESTIARY

UURGU — CR 4

XP 1,200

Female lizardfolk inquisitor of Hshurha 4 (*Pathfinder RPG Bestiary* 195, *Pathfinder RPG Advanced Player's Guide* 38)

NE Medium humanoid (reptilian)

Init +4; **Senses** Perception +9

DEFENSE

AC 20, touch 12, flat-footed 18 (+3 armor, +2 Dex, +5 natural)

hp 37 (6d8+10)

Fort +9, **Ref** +4, **Will** +7

DR 1/magic

OFFENSE

Speed 30 ft., swim 15 ft.

Melee *+1 quarterstaff* +10 (1d6+6), bite +3 (1d4+2) or *+1 quarterstaff* +8 (1d6+5), *+1 quarterstaff* +8 (1d6+5), bite +3 (1d4+2)

Special Attacks judgment 2/day

Domain Spell-Like Abilities (CL 4th; concentration +6)

5/day—*touch of evil* (2 rounds)

Inquisitor Spell-Like Abilities (CL 4th; concentration +6)

At will—*detect alignment*

Inquisitor Spells Known (CL 4th; concentration +6)

2nd (2/day)—*death knell* (DC 14), *silence* (DC 14)

1st (4/day)—*alarm*, *cause fear* (DC 13), *divine favor*, *magic weapon*

0 (at will)—*bleed* (DC 12), *detect magic*, *guidance*, *read magic*, *resistance*, *virtue*

Domain Evil

TACTICS

Before Combat Uurgu casts *alarm* on area **N16** each day, and if alerted to intruders, casts *divine favor* on herself and *magic weapon* on her staff.

During Combat Uurgu offers intruders one chance to surrender (for later sacrifice to the elemental lord she worships) before declaring her judgment of resiliency and launching into combat. She targets enemy divine casters with *silence*, then attacks with her staff. If one of her cultists falls, she slays him with *death knell*.

Morale Uurgu fights to the death.

Base Statistics Without *divine favor* and *magic weapon* cast, Uurgu's statistics are **Melee** quarterstaff +9 (1d6+4), bite +3 (1d4+1), or quarterstaff +7 (1d6+3), quarterstaff +7 (1d6+3), bite +2 (1d4+1).

STATISTICS

Str 16, **Dex** 15, **Con** 12, **Int** 10, **Wis** 14, **Cha** 8

Base Atk +4; **CMB** +8; **CMD** 19

Feats Double Slice, Precise Strike[APG], Two-weapon Fighting, Weapon Focus (quarterstaff)

Skills Acrobatics +6, Heal +9, Intimidate +6, Knowledge (planes) +7, Knowledge (religion) +7, Perception +9, Sense Motive +11, Stealth +9, Survival +7, Swim +11; **Racial Modifiers** +4 Acrobatics

Languages Polyglot

SQ hold breath, monster lore +2, solo tactics, stern gaze +2, track +2

Combat Gear potion of cure moderate wounds, potion of darkvision, salve of slipperiness; **Other Gear** mwk studded leather, mwk quarterstaff, *cloak of resistance +1*, manacles, gold holy symbol of Hshurha (worth 60 gp)

DISCIPLES OF DARK WATER (2) — CR 2

XP 600 each

hp 20 each (see page 51)

LADY FAFRAIL — CR 5

XP 1,600

Female djinni (*Pathfinder RPG Bestiary* 139)

hp 52 (currently 42)

Development: Freeing Lady Fafrail from her prison severs the elemental tether here, just like destroying or deactivating a *storm seed* elsewhere in the complex. Freeing the genie immediately ends the torrent of wind filling this chamber.

Lady Fafrail is grateful if released, but unaccustomed to dealing with mortals. She's disgusted that she was captured—and subsequently released—by "lesser beings." Hospitable regardless, she offers her rescuers food and wine once Uurgu and her cultists are slain, along with whatever treasures they might enjoy that her *major creation* can produce (though only gifts made from plant matter last more than a few hours).

Lady Fafrail despises the Material Plane, but remains long enough to allows the PCs to ask her questions. She knows of Daruthek, Chitauli, and the lizardfolk cult, and has surmised the purpose of the complex and her entrapment, but knows little of the temple's history. If the PCs seem lost, she recalls Daruthek gloating over conjuring her to replace a damaged magic item called a *storm seed*, and suggests that shutting down or destroying the remaining orbs may shut down the storm engine. Thanks to her connection to the engine, she knows how many *storm seeds* remain, and that Daruthek currently directs the growing hurricane from the Chancel of Four Winds located inside the swirling maelstrom at the dungeon's center.

Treasure Before leaving, Lady Fafrail offers polite PCs a reward: an *air elemental gem* which summons forth one of her servants.

N18. Singing Tunnels

This smooth tunnel widens as it curves to the north; the southeast end narrows and branches into countless smaller channels.

These tubes channel the elemental energy from the choral hall (area **N17**) into the center of the storm engine. The strange shapes and passageways create the haunting music that is heard throughout the complex. As the tubes travel east, they grow too narrow for anyone to crawl through them.

N19. Chancel of Four Winds (CR 9)

The bodies of four small lizardfolk lie atop altars set in the cardinal directions of this massive, gear-shaped platform that rises from the water. Lines of strange script mark the floors, which are otherwise polished to a mirrorlike sheen.

This is the casting area for the vile Storm Kindler ritual. Protected by a column of churning wind and water while the storm engine functions, the chancel can be accessed only before or after the storms it creates, or if the primary caster within willingly opens a portal in the elemental wall. Only by destroying each of the tethers does this central platform become accessible.

On each of the four altars dedicated to the elemental lords lies the body of a lizardfolk child—necessary sacrifices to begin the corrupt ritual.

Creatures: Swamp-Speaker Daruthek floats in the center of this platform, flanked by a quartet of his cultists and a pair of elemental wysps sent to him personally—he believes—by the demigod Hshurha. Daruthek is immediately aware once the last elemental tether is destroyed, and expects the PCs to come for a final showdown, which he is eager to undertake. Daruthek knows that he is the chosen servant of two elemental lords, and seeks to use the powers gifted to him to destroy the PCs, jury-rig replacements for the *storm seeds* as he did with the djinni Lady Fafrail, and complete the final stages of the ritual.

Daruthek's air wysps remain close, adding a +2 competence bonus to all his attack and damage rolls thanks to their resonance ability (not included in the statistics below). Additionally, each time Daruthek falls below 25 hit points, an air wysp sacrifices itself using its living battery ability to restore 14 hit points to him.

DARUTHEK	CR 6

XP 2,400

Male air-infused lizardfolk oracle 5 (*Advanced Bestiary* 139, *Pathfinder RPG Bestiary* 195, *Pathfinder RPG Advanced Player's Guide* 42,

NE Medium humanoid (reptilian)

Init +1; **Senses** blindsight 30 ft., Perception +1

DEFENSE

AC 25, touch 13, flat-footed 24 (+7 armor, +2 deflection, +1 Dex, +5 natural)

hp 50 (7d8+19)

Fort +7, **Ref** +6, **Will** +9

Immune fatigue

OFFENSE

Speed 20 ft. (15 ft. in armor), fly 30 ft. (perfect), swim 15 ft.

Melee +1 spear +7 (1d8+4/×3), bite +1 (1d4+1)

Ranged light crossbow +5 (1d8/19–20)

Spell-Like Abilities (CL 5th; concentration +9)

1/day—*gaseous form*

Oracle Spells Known (CL 5th; concentration +9)

2nd (5/day)—*cure moderate wounds, gust of wind* (DC 16), *resist energy, sound burst* (DC 16)

1st (7/day)—*alter winds*ᴬᴾᴳ (DC 15), *cause fear* (DC 15), *cure light wounds, inflict light wounds* (DC 15), *obscuring mist, protection from good*

0 (at will)—*bleed* (DC 14), *create water, detect magic, detect poison, guidance, read magic*

Mystery wind

TACTICS

Before Combat Daruthek casts *protection from good* and drinks a *potion of bull's strength* once the *storm seeds* are destroyed and the storm engine's barrier falls.

During Combat Daruthek uses his lightning breath early to target opponents before his cultists close to melee, then relies on *sound burst* and flyby attacks with his spear to harry small groups of enemies. If his cultists die, he uses *obscuring mist* to blind opponents, relying on his blindsight to target them with attacks. The oracle keeps a *cause fear* spell in his *+1 spell-storing breastplate*, and targets the first creature who strikes him in melee.

Morale Daruthek and his minions fight to the death.

Base Statistics Without a *potion of bull's strength* or casting protection from good, Daruthek statistics are **AC** 23 (touch 11, flat-footed 22); **Fort** +5, **Ref** +4, **Will** +7, *+1 spear* +5 (1d8+1/×3), bite −1 (1d4); **Str** 10; **CMB** +4, **CMD** 15; **Skills** Swim +5.

STATISTICS

Str 14, **Dex** 12, **Con** 13, **Int** 10, **Wis** 12, **Cha** 18

Base Atk +4; **CMB** +6; **CMD** 19

Feats Flyby Attack, Iron Will, Lightning Reflexesᴮ, Toughness

Skills Acrobatics +2 (−6 when jumping), Diplomacy +12, Fly +14, Knowledge (planes) +7, Knowledge (religion) +7, Linguistics +1, Spellcraft +7, Stealth +2, Swim +7; **Racial Modifiers** +4 Acrobatics

Languages Auran, Polyglot

SQ hold breath, oracle's curse (lame), revelations (invisibility, lightning breath)

Combat Gear *potion of bull's strength* (2), *potion of cure moderate wounds* (2); **Other Gear** *+1 spell-storing breastplate*, *+1 spear*, light crossbow with 20 bolts

SPECIAL ABILITIES

Air Mastery (Ex) Airborne creatures take a −1 penalty on attack rolls and damage rolls against Daruthek.

Elemental Body (Ex) Each time Daruthek is subject to bleed damage, precision damage, poison, paralysis, sleep, or a stunning effect, there is a 25% chance that the effect or additional damage is negated.

INTRODUCTION

CHAPTER 1:
THE DELUGE

CHAPTER 2:
BEYOND THE COLONY

CHAPTER 3:
THE SKY TEMPEST TEMPLE

APPENDIX 1:
PRIDON'S HEARTH

APPENDIX 2:
BESTIARY

Wind Blast (Su) Once every 1d4 rounds, Daruthek can breathe a 60-foot cone of wind. Every creature within this area that is not flying must succeed at a DC 14 Acrobatics or Strength check or fall prone. A flying creature that fails is instead blown away from Daruthek, moving a distance equal to 5 feet per point by which it failed the check. If the creature encounters a large object during this movement, it takes 1d6 points of damage per 5 feet the object prevented it from moving. The save DC is Constitution-based.

AIR WYSP (2)	CR 2

XP 600 each

hp 19 (*Pathfinder RPG Bestiary 5* 282)

DISCIPLES OF DARK WATER (4)	CR 2

XP 600 each

hp 20 each (see page 51)

Development: While destroying the *storm seeds* denies the storm engine much of its power—reducing the hurricane to a powerful thunderstorm—the thunderstorm persists until Daruthek's defeat.

Treasure: Daruthek and his cult have divided the wealth they scavenged from the temple between the four altars. Altogether, it amounts to 223 pp, 1,366 gp, 7,921 sp, 10 +1 *darts*, a large saltwater pearl (worth 150 gp), three polished amber gems containing strange, hairlike feathers (worth 75 gp each), an onyx remora statue (worth 50 gp), and the skull of a roc filigreed with silver (worth 450 gp).

Story Award: Once the PCs defeat Daruthek and end the ritual, award them an additional 6,400 XP.

Concluding the Adventure

Within hours of Daruthek's death, the clouds surrounding the region begin to break apart, and beams of sunshine warm the land. The floodwaters recede. For the next several days, the sky remains a perfect blue, bereft of clouds, rain, or thunder. Soon enough the weather returns to normal in the region, as all traces of the elemental intrusion are over. With the ritual ended, the elemental lords Hshurha and Kelizandri revoke their blessings from the temple, and much of the lower level of the temple collapses in the coming days and months.

If the PCs killed Chief Shathva, the remaining Mireborn retreat for now, but in the coming years become an ongoing menace to Pridon's Hearth, raiding the outlying farms. If the PCs brokered a peaceful resolution with Chief Shathva, the Mireborn remain in the area but abandon the Sky Tempest Temple. In this case, the lizardfolk are eager to claim a new homeland, and expect the PCs to continue aiding them in peaceful negotiations with the human colonists.

Count Narsus pays his promised rewards to the PCs, and officially inducts the PCs into the town council to help oversee the community's growth and protection (should they desire). The count also sees the PCs as a "civic treasure," and creates a holiday in their honor. Furthermore, he grants a parcel of land to each PC (including areas the PCs may have visited during their adventure, such as the Ghol-Gan ruin or the tar pit).

If GMs wish to continue adventuring around Pridon's Hearth, the storms may have dredged up all manner of monsters, from agitated wildlife to inhabitants of other Ghol-Gan ruins to krakens or aboleths attracted to the unnatural storm's power. The ritual may have even stranded creatures from the Elemental Planes just as the first Storm Kindler ritual trapped Guuhgwa, leading to new threats or refugees seeking aid. The PCs could also assist the Mireborn in negotiating with or settling in or near Pridon's Hearth, or assist the lizardfolk in reclaiming their home from the boggard invaders.

DARUTHEK

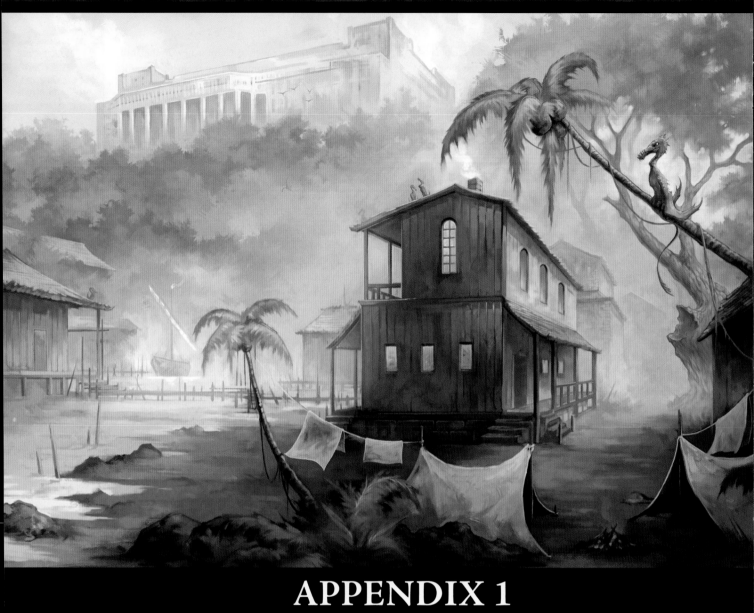

APPENDIX 1

Pridon's Hearth

Originally named "Pridon's Grave" by the local Song'o halfling tribes, and often called "Pridon's Folly" in Sargava proper, the upstart colonial town of Pridon's Hearth represents the wayward Chelish colony's latest attempt to expand its borders and establish itself as an international power. A Sargavan entrepreneur named Rema Pridon made what she hoped would be a historic journey in 4622 AR. She chartered a ship, brought almost four dozen followers, and made the journey south to explore the Jungle of Hungry Trees and uncover gold mines that existed only in her imagination. A disastrous tale followed when Pridon's ship washed ashore, stranding the entrepreneur and her surviving followers along the Lower Korir River delta's marshy but fertile coast. Pridon and the other refugees managed to survive for just over 5 years—battling the jungle's dinosaurs and other monsters—before eventually succumbing to malaria.

A tribe of Song'o halflings eventually discovered the site of Pridon's landing and camp, passing the information on to Sargavan officials during their brief contact with colonials decades later. Servius Narsus—a merchant with dreams of nobility—caught wind of the fertile territory around the camp, and bartered for a stake in the land. General Septimia Arodatus—known for handing out territorial claims she has no right to grant—eagerly accepted Narsus's request, installing the merchant as the region's count. As a condition of his appointment, Narsus's title and claims would be recognized in Sargava proper only if he could tame and then annex the wilderness territory into the larger colony.

The first ships set sail 4 years ago, and the freshly appointed Count Narsus dubbed the settlement "Pridon's Hearth" after mistranslating the local name for the collection of islands at the river's mouth. Newly widowed, Count Narsus brought along his only heir—his son Lethar—as well as their entire familial contingent of slaves. Narsus declared his slaves free men and women as his first act upon establishing the settlement; to Narsus, this decree reinforced his command that Pridon's Hearth should be a new start for any who seeks one—it also cleverly absolved him of any responsibility for the former slaves' survival in the harsh terrain. Many of the count's soldiers feared mass dereliction or rebellion, but Narsus's generosity won through, and most of the freed slaves stayed to help establish the settlement.

Narsus lived just long enough to see his settlement take root. Only a year after first landing, Narsus fell victim to malaria, just as the town's namesake had decades ago. Lethar Narsus took his father's mantle, becoming the region's count and devoting himself to his father's principles. Just months after the elder Narsus's death, explorers discovered the native fever tree, whose bark can be prepared into a tonic to ward off tropical diseases; the cultivation of the bark quickly became the center of the settlement's economy. With this prospective cash crop in hand, Lethar dispatched messengers to Eleder, and even further north to the nations of the Inner Sea region, announcing his plans to expand the settlement. This message promised land and legacies for those willing to work on behalf of Sargava's interests in the region. Today, Lethar's missive has met with mixed results, bringing in numerous workers to help establish the town while simultaneously earning the attention of criminals and exploiters, most notably the Aspis Consortium.

Locals have dubbed their branch of the Lower Korir River the Little Tiger River, after the aggressive and delicious tigerfish that lurk in the waters, but they agree on few other names for local features. Though 4 years old, Pridon's Hearth remains very much a struggling colony town, with no paved roads and many buildings still constructed with canvas roofs or walls. Its residents are a mixed lot; most are stark individualists looking for a home removed from Sargava's crowded cities or opportunists hoping to uncover hidden treasures or valuable minerals in the largely unexplored river delta. For now, the town population contains few families, and even fewer people looking to start one.

Aside from the bark of the fever tree, most of the local economy depends on fishing and harvesting rare wood from the surrounding jungle. Several wealthy settlers quickly snapped up large holdings adjacent to the town itself, clearing plantations to grow various cash crops, but the harsh summer weather has complicated attempts to farm the region. Dika and oil palm orchards are the only reliable producers, though settlers have discovered wild taro and Mwangi rice stands all along the river, and use both heavily in their meals. Many entrepreneurs journey to the far-flung outpost with get-rich-quick schemes. Just as many return home penniless, or else become permanent and struggling residents of the community.

The Aspis Consortium maintains a small cadre of operatives in Pridon's Hearth, under the command of Bronze Agent Hamsa Gadd. The Consortium's original interests leaned toward acquiring as many valuable plants as possible and establishing exclusive trade rights with any undiscovered tribes, but more recently agents have been encouraged by rumors of ruins in the surrounding jungles. Hamsa Gadd's own expertise lies in trade negotiations more than wilderness exploration, and she prefers to achieve her objectives by ingratiating herself with Count Narsus.

Island Town

Several small islands break up the flow of water from the river that runs through Pridon's Hearth. Despite the islands' minor size and muddy terrain, the earliest settlers claimed much of their usable land in the town's initial land grab. Their placement along the river makes for easy access to the Little Tiger for fishing. Sturdy, if amateurish, bridges connect most of the islands, and members of the community are well versed in safely crossing these arterial paths. Locals call the assemblage of buildings and bridges Island Town, despite the fact that it is part of Pridon's Hearth. The people of Island Town are doggedly stubborn compared to their neighbors, who they refer to as "the walled-in." Both factions share little overt animosity toward one another, though residents of Island Town generally consider themselves the true residents of Pridon's Hearth.

PRIDON'S HEARTH

N small town

Corruption +2; **Crime** –3; **Economy** +0; **Law** +3; **Lore** +2; **Society** –2

Qualities insular, racially intolerant (Ekujae elves)

Danger +0

DEMOGRAPHICS

Government overlord

Population 331 (257 humans, 52 halflings, 12 half-elves, 10 other)

Notable NPCs

Advisor Hamsa Gadd (NE female human bard 4/rogue 2)

Banker Baldra Siferth (LN female venerable human cleric of Abadar 7)

Count Lethar Narsus (N male human aristocrat 4/magus[UM] 1)

Sheriff Adaela Praet (LN female human ex-paladin of Iomedae 3)

MARKETPLACE

Base Value 1,000 gp; **Purchase Limit** 5,000 gp; **Spellcasting** 4th

Minor Items 3d4; **Medium Items** 1d6; **Major Items** —

Pridon's Hearth

0 ——— 150
FEET

Notable Locations

Pridon's Hearth has numerous unique locations and residents both in the walled-in city and on the nearby islets.

1. Countinghouse of Abadar: While most frontier towns dedicate their first major church to Erastil, this settlement's church of Abadar helped fund the initial colonial petition. It earned a valuable place in the outpost, both as the initial major temple and as its exclusive financier and bank. The temple's worshipers constructed a grand edifice of stone and wood to honor their deity, hoping to become a civilizing example to their fellow settlers. Baldra Siferth remains the only full-time priest in the community, overseeing a dozen part-time acolytes and two clerics-in-training. The aged cleric uses the temple to offer healing and financial services, but she relies heavily on the town guard for protection from the rougher denizens of Pridon's Hearth.

2. Heri's Conservatorium: Local remedies and minor potions are available from **Heri Lightstep** (CN female halfling expert 3/alchemist[APG] 1), the lucky halfling who guaranteed her fortune when she discovered the fever tree. Heri also enjoys the substances she sells, particularly the alchemical secretions of jungle spiders she keeps in captivity. She can create potions of any 1st-level spell, though there's a 25% chance the creation contains some hallucinogenic ingredients, causing creatures that imbibe it to be confused for 1 round (Fortitude DC 13 negates). Heri's self-medication makes her an easy-going salesperson, and she offers all of her potions at 80% of the market value.

3. The Holdinghouses: Count Narsus owns this quartet of warehouses, and he leases the individual pens within to various shipping companies or locals who need to store provisions seasonally. The count stockpiles various supplies and equipment in a smaller warehouse nearby as part of his ever-delayed plan to expand the docks.

4. Little Tiger Docks: Pridon's Hearth currently lacks a proper dock for larger ships, instead requiring smaller skiffs to come ashore on Island Town to deliver goods. Plans to dredge the river and construct a larger dock exist, but remain unsettled as residents of Island Town constantly bicker over whose fishing will be ruined by the construction and sudden influx of larger vessels.

5. Narsus Estate: The relative grandeur of the Narsus Estate humbles the rest of Pridon's Hearth. Servant quarters, a large barn, and a boathouse sit alongside the large manor, with much of the town dedicated to the cultivation of fever trees, which young Count Narsus hopes will become the colony's main trade good. The Narsus Estate currently houses the count's advisor, Hamsa Gadd, and three of her secretaries. Unknown to the trusting young man, all of his guests are agents of the

INTRODUCTION

CHAPTER 1:
THE DELUGE

CHAPTER 2:
BEYOND THE COLONY

CHAPTER 3:
THE SKY TEMPEST TEMPLE

APPENDIX 1:
PRIDON'S HEARTH

APPENDIX 2:
BESTIARY

Aspis Consortium, tasked with turning the colony into a client-state of the amoral merchant company.

6. Narsus Forest: Four members of the count's staff have disappeared over the past month in the thick jungle abutting the town, and Count Narsus has declared the woods surrounding his estate off limits. An exceptionally large troll named **Graular** (see page 17) is responsible for these disappearances. When the troll tried to break into the dock storage yard, guards repelled the creature, but not before she ripped off a metal bar and began using it as an improvised club. With this dangerous predator newly armed, the young count has become increasingly wary of leaving his estate, especially after dark.

7. Northwind Smithy: The blacksmith shop in Pridon's Hearth has changed ownership almost a dozen times since the town's founding. **Vethorn Valgardson** (N male half-elf expert 3/fighter 1)—a strapping, no-nonsense half-elf from the distant north—currently runs the shop. Brusque and antisocial, Vethorn prefers the solace of an empty forge and ringing anvil. He crafts and repairs equipment of all types, but supplying the guard and paranoid citizens with weapons and armor occupies the majority of his time.

8. Penbury Printing: One of the town's newest additions is a fully functional printing press, operated by **Lizba Penbury** (LN female human expert 3). Lizba lost the use of her legs as a child after being run over by a carriage, and pursued her budding interest in books and mechanisms to occupy her mind during her long recovery. Though still unable to walk, she travels around town daily using a variety of wagons and crutches of her own design. The press mostly publishes tide schedules, almanacs, and public notices, but Lizba also publishes a weekly, single-page broadsheet with local gossip, news from Sargava, weather reports, and various puzzles.

9. Pridon's Masonry: Stonemason **Zander Carr** (LN male human expert 3) has spent his life working with stone; he hails from a quarry owned by a Sargavan noble. He made his way to Pridon's Hearth with a sizable amount of white marble, and has since founded the town's limestone quarry several miles south. Zander employs two dozen townsfolk as quarry workers and masons. Most buildings in town are built from wood from the surrounding jungles, rather than stone; while he dreams of someday constructing an elaborate town hall or cathedral to elevate the fledgling community's architecture, he dedicates most of his time to (and makes the most profit from) maintaining the town's defensive walls.

10. Quentin's Prognostications: Sargava tried and convicted **Artimis Quentin** (LE male human oracle[APG] 2) 2 years ago, then sent him to Pridon's Hearth to work off his debt to society. Count Narsus has allowed him to do so by making observations and predictions about the weather, which the count distributes freely to residents and the surrounding plantations. Quentin supplements his miserable allowance by offering largely fraudulent oracular services to other locals, speaking to their departed loved ones or advising people on business deals. The oracle also runs card games and sells cheap booze from his home. Quentin failed to foresee the current storms; he is desperate to find someone else to blame for the situation before the count decides he would be more valuable as a common laborer rather than in his current, relatively comfortable position.

11. Oyin Emporium: This well-kept wooden building houses items of varied description. The cantankerous proprietor, **Mirya Oyin** (NG female old human expert 4), oversees the emporium. Her late wife originally dealt with customers while Mirya handled accounts and the importing of goods. Now, Mirya juggles both sets of duties, hurling invectives at customers and rarely opening up to others, but her relative charm and well-concealed charitable nature keep her shop popular. Even those who don't appreciate Mirya's harsh demeanor know that she remains the best option for importing hard-to-find goods or shipping anything back to Sargava.

12. The Stone Hall: The first stone building in Pridon's Hearth—beating out the Temple of Abadar by several weeks—the Stone Hall operates as the town's favorite tavern and only inn. People from all over the colony come to the Stone Hall to talk and drink, or to hold semi-formal gatherings. Servius Narsus's newly freed halfling slaves constructed the building, scaling the main hall to accommodate an average human's stature while crafting several offshoot rooms more appropriate for their size. The Whithermoot and Longroad families jointly control the hall.

13. The Watched Row: Far removed from sight, Pridon's Hearth makes an appealing dumping ground for Sargava's criminal element and unruly slaves. This section of town serves as an unofficial prison colony, housing those sentenced to slavery and working off their debt to the state in Pridon's Hearth. The authorities are loose with the regulation of such prisoners and don't bother to cage them. Everyone knows there's nowhere for escapees to go—unless the prisoners plan on testing their survival skills in the harsh jungle and braving the vicious lizardfolk and boggard tribes to the north.

14. Wymackie Lumber: With most of the growing town built from wood, the lumber industry is quite profitable, and the reigning queen of trees in Pridon's Hearth is **Martel Wymackie** (CN female human rogue 1/warrior 3). Martel and her expansive family, all lumberjacks and soldiers by trade, arrived with the first colony ship and wasted no time making themselves indispensable to the earliest colonists. Though productive, Wymackie Lumber remains a hazardous place to work—Martel herself has lost a leg and four fingers to the job—and many residents of Pridon's Hearth have mixed feelings about her plan to open a sawmill in the near future.

APPENDIX 2: BESTIARY

Eaisge

Water gushes from the mouth and nose of this bloated creature. Broken wood and jagged nails jut from its half-rotted flesh.

EAISGE	CR 1

XP 400

NE Medium undead (aquatic)

Init +0; **Senses** darkvision 60 ft.; Perception +3

DEFENSE

AC 12, touch 10, flat-footed 12 (+2 natural)

hp 16 (3d8+3)

Fort +2, **Ref** +1, **Will** +4

DR 5/piercing or slashing; **Immune** undead traits; **Resist** cold 5, fire 5

OFFENSE

Speed 30 ft.

Melee slam +4 (1d8+3)

Ranged gush +2 (1d4+2 plus trip)

Special Attacks create spawn, embedded debris, gush

STATISTICS

Str 15, **Dex** 10, **Con** —, **Int** 6, **Wis** 8, **Cha** 13

Base Atk +2; **CMB** +4; **CMD** 14

Feats Blind-Fight, Iron Will

Skills Intimidate +6, Perception +3, Stealth +5 (+9 underwater), Swim +6; **Racial Modifiers** +4 Stealth underwater

Languages Aquan

ECOLOGY

Environment any swamp or water

Organization solitary, pair, or wreck (3–15)

Treasure standard

SPECIAL ABILITIES

Create Spawn (Su) As a full-round action, an eaisge can expel water from its mouth onto a creature it has killed in the past minute. A humanoid creature with fewer than 3 Hit Dice bathed in these putrid waters rises as a zombie 1d4 rounds later. A humanoid with 3 Hit Dice or more rises as a new eaisge, though these newly formed eaisge lack the embedded debris special ability for the first 24 hours. An eaisge has no ability to control the undead it creates.

Embedded Debris (Ex) Large chunks of flotsam are embedded in an eaisge's body, increasing the undead's slam damage. This debris can be sundered as if it were a held weapon (hardness 5, 10 hp), but not disarmed. If an eaisge's debris is destroyed, the eaisge's slam damage is reduced to 1d4 + its Strength modifier for 24 hours while its body recollects debris.

Gush (Ex) An eaisge can spew a gout of putrid water from its mouth as a standard action, targeting a single creature within 30 feet with this ranged touch attack. If this attack hits, it deals damage as a thrown weapon (as indicated above), and the eaisge can attempt to trip its target as a free action that does not provoke an attack of opportunity. If the attempt fails by 10 or more, the eaisge isn't knocked prone.

Eaisges form in the aftermath of torrential storms linked to the Elemental Planes, especially the Plane of Water. Extraplanar energies warp and twist the mortal souls of those claimed in these disasters, and this eventually animates their bloated corpses as horrid mockeries of life. Eaisges resemble their living forms, but with bloated bodies that drip rancid water and their skin pruned into repulsive folds. They weigh twice what they did in life thanks to this saturation.

These horrible creatures may lie dormant and harmless for months or years before suddenly exploding with terrible purpose. Eaisges naturally attract bits of flotsam and debris. Their bodies absorb this refuse, wrapping their limbs around driftwood and rubble—this causes the constant pain that inspires their outrage and bursts of violence.

Mamiwa

The tail of this shimmering, salamander-like creature is composed entirely of water.

MAMIWA   **CR 2**

XP 600

N Tiny outsider (air, elemental, native, water)

Init +2; **Senses** darkvision 60 ft.; Perception +7

DEFENSE

AC 15, touch 15, flat-footed 12 (+2 Dex, +1 dodge, +2 size)

hp 19 (3d10+3)

Fort +4, **Ref** +5, **Will** +2

Immune elemental traits; **Resist** cold or electricity 5

Weaknesses vulnerable to fire

OFFENSE

Speed 20 ft., fly 50 ft. (perfect), swim 50 ft.

Melee bite +7 (1d3–2)

Ranged elemental blast +7 (2d6 cold or electricity)

Space 2-1/2 ft.; **Reach** 0 ft.

Special Attacks elemental blast, elemental infusion

STATISTICS

Str 7, **Dex** 15, **Con** 12, **Int** 10, **Wis** 12, **Cha** 13

Base Atk +3; **CMB** +3; **CMD** 12 (can't be tripped)

Feats Dodge, Weapon Finesse

Skills Acrobatics +8 (+0 when jumping), Fly +20, Knowledge (nature) +6, Perception +7, Survival +7 (+11 to predict the weather), Swim +12; **Racial Modifiers** –8 Acrobatics when jumping, +4 Survival to predict the weather

Languages Common; rain speaker, *speak with animals*

SQ elemental alignment

ECOLOGY

Environment any

Organization solitary or stormfront (2–12)

Treasure incidental

SPECIAL ABILITIES

Elemental Alignment (Su) Each day at sunrise, a mamiwa must align itself toward either air or water. An air-aligned mamiwa gains electricity resistance 5, its elemental blast and elemental infusion abilities deal electricity damage, and it gains Auran as a bonus language. A mamiwa aligned with water instead gains cold resistance 5, deals cold damage with its attacks, and gains Aquan as a bonus language.

Elemental Blast (Su) A mamiwa can unleash a blast of elemental energy as a ranged touch attack.

Creatures struck by this blast take 2d6 points of cold or electricity damage, depending on the mamiwa's elemental alignment for that day.

Elemental Infusion (Su) As a standard action, a mamiwa can join itself with a single weapon or suit of armor. A mamiwa cannot act while infusing an object, except to end the infusion, but does impart some of its elemental nature to whatever it inhabits. An infused weapon deals an additional 1d6 points of energy damage, while an infused suit of armor instead grants both the armor and its wearer energy resistance 5. The energy type of this bonus damage and resistance depends on the mamiwa's elemental alignment for that day. Each day, a mamiwa can maintain its elemental infusion for up to 1 minute per Hit Die. This time does not need to be consecutive, but must be used in 1-minute increments. If the infused object is destroyed, the mamiwa immediately appears adjacent to the wearer and is staggered for 1d6 rounds.

Rain Speaker (Ex) A mamiwa gains telepathy out to 100 feet in any sort of precipitation, but can communicate only with other creatures that are also being rained upon.

When powerful storms roll across the Material Plane, the elemental morass of air and water sometimes births mamiwas—curious and frantic little spirits of temperamental weather. Clever despite their animalistic appearance, they love investigating new sights and sounds, and find buildings made by humanoids endlessly fascinating. Many follow storms, and unwittingly cause extraordinary amounts of damage as they tear holes in roofs or clog drains just as the rainfall reaches its peak. They love silver—which reminds them of rainfall—and can be easily bribed into abandoning their mischief for a handful of coins.

Because they're fragile and lack an intrinsic link to the Elemental Planes to bind them together, mamiwas must rest by binding themselves into solid objects each day to maintain their forms, or else they must dedicate themselves to a greater power and beg enough elemental energy to remain coherent. Many find succor in Gozreh, but a few malicious mamiwas follow the elemental lords Hshurha or Kelizandri instead. Mamiwas can also obtain the energy they need to survive from mortal mages, and a neutral-aligned 7th-level spellcaster who has the Improved Familiar feat can gain a mamiwa as a familiar.

INTRODUCTION

CHAPTER 1:
THE DELUGE

CHAPTER 2:
BEYOND THE COLONY

CHAPTER 3:
THE SKY TEMPEST TEMPLE

APPENDIX 1:
PRIDON'S HEARTH

APPENDIX 2:
BESTIARY

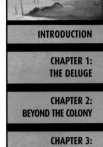